Beginner's ARABIC Script

John Mace

TEACH YOURSELF BOOKS

For UK order queries: please contact Bookpoint Ltd, 78 Milton Park, Abingdon, Oxon OX14 4TD. Telephone: (44) 01235 400414, Fax: (44) 01235 400454. Lines are open from 9.00–6.00, Monday to Saturday, with a 24 hour message answering service. Email address: orders@bookpoint.co.uk

For USA & Canada order queries: please contact NTC/Contemporary Publishing, 4255 West Touhy Avenue, Lincolnwood, Illinois 60646–1975, USA. Telephone: (847) 679 5500, Fax: (847) 679 2494.

Long renowned as the authoritative source for self-guided learning – with more than 40 million copies sold worldwide – the *Teach Yourself* series includes over 200 titles in the fields of languages, crafts, hobbies, business and education.

British Library Cataloguing in Publication Data
A catalogue record for this title is available from The British Library.

Library of Congress Catalog Card Number: On file

First published in UK 1999 by Hodder Headline Plc, 338 Euston Road, London, NW1 3BH.

First published in US 1999 by NTC/Contemporary Publishing, 4255 West Touhy Avenue, Lincolnwood (Chicago), Illinois 60646–1975 USA.

Typeset by John Mace.
Printed in Great Britain for Hodder & Stoughton Educational, a division of Hodder Headline Plc, 338 Euston Road, London NW1 3BH by Cox & Wyman Ltd, Reading, Berkshire.

Impression number	10 9 8 7 6 5 4 3 2 1
Year	2005 2004 2003 2002 2001 2000 1999

Acknowledgements

I am grateful to the following organisations for their kind permission to reproduce certain original material in this book:
- Shell International Ltd. for the line drawing of a road tanker shown on p. 55, taken from their publication 'Oil for Everybody',
- Al-Hayat newspaper for the three headlines shown on p. 123,
- the Bank of Lebanon for the banknote shown on p. 124.

I am also indebted to Marilyn Moore for her indefatigable proof-reading and checking. Any errors now found in this text are my responsibility.

Books on Arabic by the same author

Arabic Today, a student, business and professional course in spoken and written Arabic, Edinburgh University Press 1996, ISBN 0 7486 0616 5
Arabic Grammar, A Reference Guide, Edinburgh University Press 1998, ISBN 0 7486 1079 0
Teach Yourself Arabic Verbs and Essential Grammar, Hodder & Stoughton 1999, ISBN 0 340 73008 0

CONTENTS

Introduction

Reading and writing Arabic. The Arabic alphabet.
How to use this book 1

1 **ا alif, آ alif madda, ب bā, ت tā, ث <u>th</u>ā, ن nūn, ي yā**. Stress. 5

2 **ل lām, م mīm, و wow**. Doubled letters. ّ **<u>sh</u>adda**. Definite article. 14

3 **ء hamza, ه hā, ة tā marbūṭa**. Feminine forms. **س sīn, ش <u>sh</u>īn**. 23

4 **ر rā, ز zayy, د dāl, ذ <u>dh</u>āl, ص ṣād, ض ḍād**. Dark sounds. Relatives. 32

5 **ج jīm, ح ḥā, خ <u>kh</u>ā, ط ṭā, ظ ẓā, ع 9ayn, غ <u>gh</u>ayn**. Stress. 40

6 **ف fā, ق qāf, ك kāf. اً\ةً tanwīn, ى alif maqṣūra**. Full alphabet. Arabic transcription. 48

7 Dual. Regular plural. Irregular plural. Figures. 57

8 Participles. Verbal nouns. Abstract nouns. Other written styles. 66

9 New words: *Communications* 73
Basic structures, 1: The Description. Possessive.

10 New words: *Work*. Personal pronouns. 84
Basic structures, 2: The Equation.

11 New words: *Town*. Prepositions. Command form. 91

12 New words: *Administration*. 99
Basic structures, 3: The Construct.

13 New words: *Time and Money*. Numbers. Clock. Calendar. 109

14 New words: *The Arab World*. Map. 118

15 Test your reading: Signs, Headlines, Small print, Handwriting. 122

Key to Tests 127

Arabic-English Vocabulary 135

English-Arabic Vocabulary 154

Index 167

Pocket Card Alphabet. Nouns and Adjectives. 169
Command Form, Participles, Verbal nouns. Figures.

INTRODUCTION

Reading and writing Arabic

Arabic writing seems daunting at first sight, but it doesn't have to be. This book attempts to take the mystique out of it. You learn the alphabet in stages, practising each new letter or combination of letters many times before moving on to the next; at the same time you fit the letters into useful words and phrases seen everywhere in any Arab environment.

This book is actual; you learn to read and write today's Arabic. And you learn through practice, from the start.

That said, nobody can promise that when you have finished this book you'll be able to read a newspaper article, or write a report. That requires a knowledge of Arabic grammar going beyond our immediate scope. But you will be able to read and understand important signs and directions - even better, you will know what sort of words to expect. You will also be able to read and understand many newspaper headlines, and to write everything you can read.

The Arabic language

Arabic is a world language. It is the official language, or one of the official languages, of nineteen countries spread across Saharan Africa and most of the Middle East. It is also one of the official languages of the United Nations. Arab culture has a high reputation, and is studied at countless universities in the western world.

Words in Arabic are built on a 'root' of three (occasionally four) consonants, which contain the basic idea underlying all the words made from the root. An example is the root consisting of the three consonants **k t b**, which has the basic idea of *writing*. From this root Arabic makes:

- the verb **katab** *to write*
- the noun **kātib** for *writer*
- **maktūb** for *written* or for *letter*
- **kitāba** for the action of *writing*
- **maktab** for *office*, or the place where one writes
- **kitāb** for *book*
- **maktaba** for *library* or *bookshop*, and so on.

The words may have bits added on, or may change internally, but you still find the three root consonants, all present and always in the same order, throughout all the derivatives.

This is of enormous help. It means that if you know one Arabic word of a particular root, you can make an intelligent guess at the meaning of a previously unknown word showing that root.

Spoken Arabic varies from place to place. It is not normally written down (there is not even an agreed way to spell it), and it is never used for formal or official written communication.

But written Arabic is the same throughout the Arab world. The Cairo newspaper **al-'ahrām** (*The Pyramids*) is read with ease in Casablanca, at the other end of North Africa. This is the Arabic found on all signs, notices, advertisements and so on, and it has a standard pronunciation. This is the form of Arabic which we are about to explore.

The Arabic alphabet

First, some essential principles on which the Arabic alphabet is based. Refer back here if you are in doubt later:

- The writing runs from right to left ← ←.
- There are no capital letters.
- Short vowels (the sounds **a** as in English *man*, **i** as in English *pin*, and **u** as in English *put*) are mostly not written; we usually have to infer them from the context.
- Printed Arabic is originally an imitation of handwriting. Most of the letters (called 'joined letters') are joined to the letter following them in the same word. A few letters ('disjoined letters') are never joined to the letter following them.

All this sounds complicated. It is not. Don't attempt to remember it now; it will become familiar as you read and write.

How to use this book

This is a participative book. You have to do a geat deal of reading and writing. You learn, and remember, by doing.

Arm yourself at the outset with a solid exercise book with lined paper. Do all your writing in this exercise book. You should also write out your vocabulary somewhere permanent, whether in the back of this exercise book, or in a different one. Writing is a powerful aid to memory.

Units 1 to 6: Alphabet

Follow the text, practising writing each new letter or group of letters as instructed. Pay attention to the notes on handwriting; there are certain important differences between handwriting and print. In the 'Read and write' parts of each unit, you see both. Imitate the handwriting for preference: you can write like printing if you wish, but it looks unnatural, and is slower. Read your writing back. Read and write everything several times.

The letters are taught in an order which helps you to build up quickly a battery of words which you can write. Any pitfalls are pointed out on the way. From letters you will move to words. Also in these units, your progress is monitored with a series of exercises at each stage; then at the end of the unit you have tests, which are more difficult than the exercises as they offer only the barest of help, and are more formal.

Don't move on to a new unit until you are at least reasonably confident about the last one - and that includes having performed well in the tests, for which you can check your answers in the key.

While following these units, don't force yourself to learn words by heart. Some will stick in your mind anyway - so much the better. The important thing is that you can by now put the letters together correctly, and decipher the written combinations which you see.

In Unit 6 you also learn to read and write the Arabic numerals.

Units 7 to 13: Words and Structures

In these units you learn to identify the different types of word, how to manipulate them, and how to link them in common and useful expressions and sentences. You will begin to read notices, signs, headlines. Units 9 to 13 start with new vocabulary, usually divided into 'essential' vocabulary, which you need to learn now because of its importance, and 'reference' vocabulary which is used for exercises and tests, but which you need not learn at this stage; examine it, and refer to it as you work through the unit. You will retain much of it through practice. In these units you will also learn related word-patterns which are a helpful feature of Arabic. These units also have exercises and tests.

Unit 14

This unit gives you some important geographical vocabulary for the Arab world, and a map.

Unit 15

Go carefully through the general reading test in this unit, checking your performance with the key and going back into the book where necessary.

Key to Tests

This is self-explanatory.

Vocabularies

The preamble to this section explains how to use these.

Index

The Index lists alphabetically all the technical topics covered (e.g. Construct, Noun, Participle), showing where each is found.

Pocket Card

This is found at the end of the book, and its use is explained there.

1

In this unit you will learn

- six common letters, with their pronunciation,
- when and how to join these letters,
- something about the 'stress' of a word,
- words which you can read and write, using the six letters.

General

Before starting this unit, be sure to read the Introduction; the section entitled 'The Arabic alphabet' is important for understanding the terms used below.

Letters

1

ا **alif**

The first and commonest letter of the alphabet is ا , called **alif**. It represents:

- at the beginning of a word: any of the *short* vowel sounds **a-**, **u-**, **i-** (like *a* in English *ant*, *u* in English *put*, and *i* in English *ink*, respectively).
- in the middle of a word, a *long* vowel sound **-ā-**. Imagine pronouncing *man*, in English, but drawing the vowel out: *ma-a-an*.
- at the end of a few words: short **-a.**

ا **alif** is a so-called 'disjoined' letter, that is, it is never joined to the following letter.

alif rests on the line of writing, but is 'tall' like a European *l*. Write this letter several times, starting at the right of the page: ....← ←

....ا......ا......ا......ا......ا......ا......ا......ا......ا......ا

ا ا ا ا ا ا ا ا ا ↓

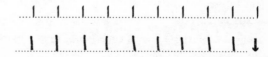

2

آ **alif madda**

alif with a stroke over it represents long **ā** (see paragraph 1 above) at the beginning of the word. This variant of **alif** is called **alif madda.**
Write this letter several times; first the downstroke, then the head:...← ←

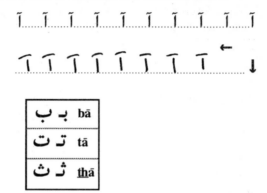

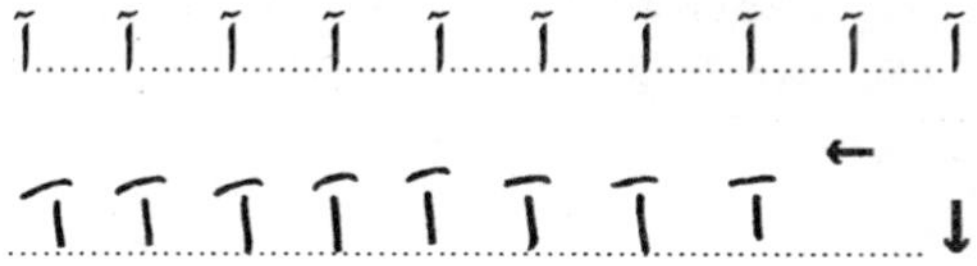

3

ب بـ	**bā**
ت تـ	**tā**
ث ثـ	**<u>th</u>ā**

The sounds **b, t** and **<u>th</u>** (soft, like *th* in *think*; the transcription is underlined to show that it is a single sound) are written respectively with the letters called **bā, tā** and **<u>th</u>ā** (see paragraph 1 for the pronunciation of **ā**). These letters are all 'shallow', i.e. they all rest on the line of writing, and are not 'tall' like **alif.**

These are 'joined' letters, that is, they are joined to any letter following them in the same word. Each letter has two possible forms: the short form is used at the beginning or in the middle of a word, and the longer form (the 'full' form) when the letter stands at the end of the word, or alone.

You will note that the three letters are identical but for the dots. These are an integral part of the letter, just as they are in English *i* or *j*. The dot(s) lie over or under the beginning of the short form, and over or under the middle of the long form. In all dotted letters the stroke is written first (← right to left), then the dot or dots.

These are the printed and typed forms. In normal handwriting, two dots usually become a dash –, and three dots something like a circumflex accent ^. Write a line of each letter, first with the dots as in print, then as in normal handwriting.

Start at the right: ....←←

بـ .... ب .... بـ .... ب .... بـ .... ب

بـ .... ب .... بـ .... ب .... بـ .... ب

تـ .... ت .... تـ .... ت .... تـ .... ت

تـ .... ت .... تـ .... ت .... تـ .... ت

ثـ .... ث .... ثـ .... ث .... ثـ .... ث

ثـ .... ث .... ثـ .... ث .... ثـ .... ث

We can now write a few words. ا is always written downwards except in its middle form, i.e. when joined to a previous letter; then it is written upwards. Remember that it is never joined to the following letter, that is, to its left. Remember also, as was said in the Introduction, that short middle and short final vowels are not normally written. Note the difference in height between **alif** (tall) and **bā-tā-thā** (shallow).

Read and write (starting at the right, remember): ←

āb *August* آب .... آ ب

ab *father** اب .... ا ب

bāb *door** باب با .... باب

athāth *furniture* اثاث .... اثاث

thābit *firm, solid* ثابت .... ثابت

* There is no word for *a* or *an* in Arabic, so for example اب **ab** means either *father* or *a father*, and باب **bāb** either *door* or *a door*.

> **Short vowel rule:** *Short vowels* (**a, i, u**) *in the middle or at the end of a word are not normally written. In a few words final* **alif** *is written for short* **-a**.

4 Stress

Think of the English word *production*; its middle vowel *u* is pronounced more strongly than the rest of the word. We say the *u* is *stressed.*

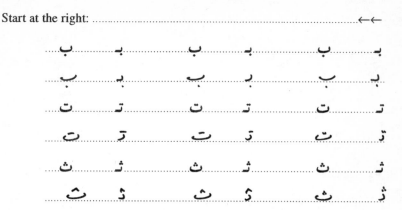

In books teaching English as a foreign language, the stress is sometimes marked with an accent (*prodúction*). We shall use this device in transcription in the first five units of this book: you see this in **a<u>th</u>ā́<u>th</u>** and **<u>th</u>ā́bit** above.

Exercise 1 Match these words with their sound and their meaning given in the list below. The first one is done for you:

(a) اب **ab** *father* (b) آب (c) اثاث (d) باب

a<u>th</u>ā́<u>th</u>, āb, bāb; *door, furniture, August.*

Exercise 2 In Exercise 1, mark the **álif**s which are pronounced long, **ā**.

Exercise 3 Write the word باب **bāb** *door*. Why is the first **bā** written differently from the last one? And why isn't the whole word joined up?

The answers to these exercises follow paragraph 6 below.

5 | ن نـ **nūn** |

We write the sound **n** with the joined letter **nūn** (**n** as in English, long **ū** like *u* in English *truth*). This letter has a short form used at the beginning or in the middle of a word, and a full form used at the end of the word, or when the letter stands alone. The dot is an integral part of the letter. The short form differs from **bā** (paragraph 3 above) only in the position of the dot, while the full form starts just above the line of writing and swoops below it and up again. We can call it a 'deep' shape. In handwriting, the dot of full-form **nūn** often takes the form of a hook on the curve itself: ن

Write several examples of **nūn**, first as in print, i.e. with a dot on the full form; then with a hook on that form as in normal handwriting:..........←←

نـ .... ن .... نـ .... ن .... نـ .... ن ....

نـ .... ن .... نـ .... ن .... نـ .... ن ....

Now ***read and write*** more words with the five letters we know (from the right):...←←

............ابن ابن **ibn** *son* ....بنت بنت **bint** *daughter, girl*

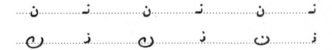

……انا انا **ána** *I* ……انت انت **ánta** *you*

……بنات بنات **banát** *daughters* ……نبات نبات **nabát** *vegetation*

Always *write* your words, don't draw or trace them. Don't grip the pen tightly, and think ahead about what you are writing, so that you anticipate which form of the coming letters you are going to use.

6

يـ ي **yā**

The 'joined' letter **yā** represents:

- at the beginning of a word: the consonant **y-** (like English *y* in *year*).
- in the middle of a word: either the consonant **-y-** (see above), or the long vowel **-ī-** (like *i* in English *machine*), or the vowel-combination **-ay-** (like *ay* in English *day*).
- at the end of a word: the long vowel **-ī** (see above).

The letter **yā** is *never* pronounced like the vowel-sound *y* in English *my*.

Like the **bā-tā-thā** group which we learned earlier, this letter has a shallow short form used at the beginning or in the middle of a word, and a full form at the end if the word, or when the letter stands alone. The short form is identical to **tā** except that its two dots are below; its full form has a deep shape and is quite different, swooping below the line and up again. Write **yā** several times, first with dots and then in the handwritten form, with a dash:……←←

يـ……ي……يـ……ي……يـ……ي

يـ……ي……يـ……ي……يـ……ي

More words. ***Read and write*** (remember that initial **yā** must be **y-**, middle **yā** can be **-y-**, **-ī-** or **-ay-**, while final **yā** is **-ī**):

……بيت بيت **bayt** *house* ……بيتين بيتين **baytáyn** *two houses*

اثنين **ithnáyn** *two* بنايات **bināyā́t** *buildings*

بنتين **bintáyn** *two daughters/girls*

In their short forms, the letters ـيـ ـنـ ـثـ ـتـ ـبـ are called ‘toothed letters’ - the form ـ is a ‘tooth’.

When full-form ي is preceded by one or more toothed letters, there are special handwritten shapes, which you should always use even if they are not present in print:

tooth + final ي: ى بي *teeth + final* ي: ى سي

Read and write:

ابي **ábī** *my father* بناتي **banā́tī** *my daughters*

ياباني **yābā́nī** *Japanese* بنتي **bíntī** *my daughter*

ابني **íbnī** *my son* بيتي **báytī** *my house*

(Remember to pronounce the stress on the vowel marked with an accent: **ábī**.)

Exercise 4 Match each of the following words with its sound and its meaning. The first one is done for you:

(a) بيت **bayt** *house* (b) بنتي (c) بنايات (d) ابني

bināyā́t, bíntī, íbnī; *buildings, my son, my daughter.*

Exercise 5 Write all the Arabic words you know which (a) begin with ا or آ, or (b) end in ي , or (c) have ن in them. Expressions with the additional meaning *my* or *two* do not count.

The answers to these exercises are given after this paragraph.

You will recall that **...يـ yā** at the beginning of the word gives the sound **y-**. We also know that initial **...ا álif** represents a short initial vowel. Note now that any word beginning with a *long* vowel or a vowel-*combination* in pronunciation must be introduced in writing by **álif**, which itself then has no sound. So initial **ī-** or **ay-** is written **...ايـ** (the **álif** being silent). ***Read and write:***

اين.....اين..... **áyna** *where*

> **Initial long vowel rule:** *Any long vowel or vowel-combination beginning a word must be introduced by* **álif** *in writing; the* **álif** *itself is then not pronounced.*

Answers to Exercises

Exercise 1 (b) آب **āb** *August*; (c) اثاث **a<u>th</u>ā́<u>th</u>** *furniture*; (d) باب **bāb** *door*.

Exercise 2 The words are are آب , اثاث and باب. The other **álifs** are short, pronounced **a**.

Exercise 3 The letter ب ـبـ **bā** has the long form at the end of the word, and the short form at the beginning or in the middle. And the word isn't joined up completely because it has to break after ا **álif** which is never joined to the next letter, i.e. it is a *disjoined* letter.

Exercise 4 (b) بنتي **bíntī** *my daughter* (c) بنايات **bināyā́t** *buildings* (d) ابني **íbnī** *my son*.

Exercise 5 The total list studied so far (in order of appearance) is:

(a) آب اب اثاث ابن انت انا اثنين اين (b) ياباني

(c) بنت ابن انت انا نبات بنات اثنين ياباني اين

If you got more than 12 out of the whole 18, you did well. If you scored below 9, it would be a good idea to re-read the unit and note what you missed.

Tests

1 Write the letters as a word. For example, (a) ب ي ت is بيت :

(a) ب ي ت (b) ب ي ت ي ن (c) ا ب ن ي

(d) ا ث ا ث ي (e) ن ب ا ت

2 Read aloud your handwritten answers to Test 1. For example, (a) is **bayt.**

3 Read aloud. For example, (a) is **banāt**:

(a) بنات (b) اثنين (c) ياباني
(d) اين (e) ابني

4 Write. For example, (a) is ابني :

(a) **ibnī** (b) **bintayn** (c) **bināyātī**
(d) **bābayn** (e) **ayna** (f) **a<u>th</u>ā<u>th</u>ī**

5 Read the words. What is the sound of each ا in each example? Explain why. For example, in (a) ابن **ibn** it is **i**, because here ا stands for the short vowel **i**:

(a) ابن (b) باب (c) آب
(d) نبات (e) اثنين

Review

In this unit we studied six letters (plus one variant), five of them extremely common. You learned

- that **álif** at the beginning or a word either stands for a *short* vowel (**a, i, u**) or introduces a *long* vowel **ī** or a *vowel-combination* **ay**,
- that **álif mádda** always represents long **ā**,
- the important difference between short and long vowels,
- that short vowels (**a, i, u**) in the middle or at the end of a word are not usually written, though final **álif** sometimes expresses short **-a**,
- the important difference between 'joined' and 'disjoined' letters,
- the difference between 'tall', 'shallow' and 'deep' written shapes,
- all the 'toothed' letters, including how to write final **yā** after a tooth and after teeth.

You have practised reading and writing joined letters (ب, ت, ث, ن, ي) in full and short forms, also taking account of tall, shallow and deep shapes.

You have read and written 22 different words out of many more which are now within your grasp.

There is a lot in this first unit; that is because with any fewer than these six letters you would get fewer than ten words, and who wants that? You have made your first encounter with this writing system which is totally different from that of any European language; don't be surprised or discouraged if it looks tough. Go back and read through the unit again, and pick up anything that baffled you the first time. Don't look for immediate perfection. Keep going; things will get clearer, and you will gain confidence, as we advance.

2

In this unit you will learn

- three more letters, also very common, with their pronunciation,
- words which you can read and write, using these letters,
- how to write doubled letters,
- how to express *the*.

Letters

1

ل ـل **lām**

The letter called **lām** represents the sound *l*. Pronounce it *light*, as in English *leaf*, not *dark* as in *wall*. **lām** looks like a European handwritten *l* written in the opposite direction. **lām** is a joined* letter; the short and full forms are used exactly like those of any other joined letter, e.g. ـب ب **bā** which we already know. However, both forms of **lām** are tall*, while the full form is also deep*, with a swoop.

* Look again at Unit 1 for the meaning of these terms, if you are unsure.

Write this letter several times: short form tall, full form both tall and deep:

.... ل .... ـل .... ل .... ـل .... ل .... ـل

.... ل .... ـل .... ل .... ـل .... ل .... ـل

You might think that **álif** and the short form of **lām** get confused; in practice this is not so. **álif** is disjoined, **lām** is joined, and there is never confusion. Look, for example, at **<u>th</u>ấli<u>th</u>** *'third'* below. Read and write:

ثالث	.... ثالث	**<u>th</u>ấli<u>th</u>** *third*	لي	.... لي	**lī** *to me, for me*
لبناني	.... لبناني	**lubnấnī** *Lebanese*	لبنان	.... لبنان	**lubnấn** *Lebanon*
			ابل	.... ابل	**íbil** *camels*

The combination **lām + álif** has special forms. In print and type, the **álif** is sloped and joins the **lām** at the latter's middle. In handwriting, we *break* the joint, and may either slope the **álif** or leave it upright. In both cases, the **álif** is written *downwards*. Look at the following forms:

	handwriting	*print and type*
not following a joined letter	لا لا	لا
following a joined letter	ـلا ـلا	ـلا

Imitate one of the handwritten forms in each case.

Read and write (choose which form you prefer):

..........ثلاث ثلاث **thaláth** *three* ....آلات آلات **ālát** *tools*

..........لا لا **la** *no*

You will never see the form (لا) in correctly written Arabic, whether in handwriting or print.

The break in the connection of **lām-álif** in handwriting does not mean that the **lām** has suddenly become a disjoined letter; it is merely a peculiarity of handwritten style.

2

م مـ **mīm**

The sound **m** (as in English *me*) is written with the letter called **mīm**. This letter is joined. Its two forms are used exactly as are the two forms of the other joined letters. Its short form is shallow, while the full form is deep with a straight downward tail. The 'bead' of both forms rests on the line of writing.

When **mim** is not joined to a preceding letter (i.e. to its right), its bead can be written clockwise or anticlockwise. Write this letter several times:

..........م..........مـ ....م..........مـ ....م..........مـ

..........م..........مـ..........م..........مـ..........م..........مـ

Read and write (the bead can go either way round):

.....من..من **min** *from* .....امام..امام **amām** *in front of*

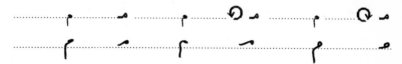

But when joined to a preceding letter, the **mim** is approached from the

top, and written *anticlockwise* ↺. This gives us special combinations after certain letters, which may or may not be used in print, but which are *always* used in handwriting. Write the handwritten forms:

	handwriting	*print and type*
tooth + **mīm**	مـ ـم	ـ\ـمـ نم
teeth + **mīm**	سم ـسم	ـسمـ سم
lām + mīm	لم ـلم	ـ\ـلمـ لم
mīm + mīm	مم ـمم	ـ\ـممـ مم

Now ***read and write:***

........تمام تمام **tamām** *perfect* ....نمل نمل **naml** *ants*

........الماني الماني **almánī** *German* ....انتم انتم **ántum** *you*

Exercise 1 Match these words with their sound and their meaning given in the list below. The first one is done for you:

(a) الماني **almánī** *German* (b) تمام (c) ثالث (d) ثلاث

<u>th</u>ālí<u>th</u>, <u>th</u>alā<u>th</u>, tamām; *perfect, third, three.*

Exercise 2 Complete the word with the right form of **lām-álif**:

no ... (c) آ...ت (b) ثـ..ث (a)

Exercise 3 The consul has got the nationalities mixed. Sort them out:

ليبي (d) لبناني (c) ياباني (b) الماني (a)

Japanese, Lebanese, Libyan, German; **almánī, líbī, yābánī, lubnánī**
(One of these words is new, but you can handle it.)

The answers to these exercises follow paragraph 5 below.

3

و **wow**

The letter called **wow** is deep and disjoined (you know what that means now). It has only one form, with a half-swoop downwards and along only, not up. Write it several times, starting with the ring written

clockwise ↻ and resting on the line of writing:

و .... و .... و .... و .... و .... و ....

و .... و .... و .... و .... و .... و ....

The letter **wow** represents the following sounds:

- at the beginning of a word: the consonant **w-** (like *w* in English *weak*).
- in the middle of a word: either the consonant **-w-** (see above), or the long vowel **-ū-** (like *u* in English *truth*), or the vowel-combinations **-ou-** (as in English *soul**) or **-ow-** (as in English *now*).
- at the end of a word: the long vowel **-ū** (see above) or, in a few words, **-ow** (see above).

The letter **wow** is *never* pronounced like *u* in English *union.*

* The pronounciation **ou** is not officially correct; the vowel-combination should sound **ow**. But in certain words even educated Arabs read it aloud as **ou** except in very formal circumstances. We shall show it as it sounds in ordinary reading aloud.

Look back to Unit 1, paragraph 6, the description of **yā**, very similar to the description given above for **wow**. Both letters are used to represent a consonant, or a long vowel, or a vowel-combination, in corresponding positions.

Read and write (remember that initial **wow** must be **w-**, middle **wow** can be **-w-**, **-ū-**, **-ou-** or **-ow-**, and final **wow** is **-ū-** or, less often, **-ow-**):

ثانوي ثانوي	**th̲ānawī** *secondary*	و ......و......	**wa** *and*
يوم ......يوم	**youm** *day*	لون ......لون	**loun** *colour*
يوليو يوليو	**yūliyū** *July*	يونيو يونيو	**yūniyū** *June*
ممنون ......ممنون	**mamnūn** *grateful*	بيوت بيوت	**buyūt** *houses*
مايو ......مايو	**māyū** *May*	تمويل تمويل	**tamwīl** *financing*

Also back in Unit 1, paragraph 6, we recorded the fact that any word beginning with a *long* vowel or a vowel-*combination* in pronunciation must be introduced in writing by **álif**, which itself then has no sound. This applies to the sounds **ū-**, **ou-** and **ow-** beginning a word: all these sounds in this situation are written **...او** (the **alif** being silent).

Read and write:

......او..او **ow** *or*

4 Doubled Letters

When we have two identical letters separated by a vowel (long or short), then we write both letters: in the word **ممنون** *grateful* (shown above) we have two examples: (**m** + *short vowel* + **m**) and (**n** + *long vowel* + **n**). Whether the vowel is short and unwritten or long and written makes no difference; there is a vowel, and the two identical letters are shown.

But when we have a *doubled letter*, i.e. two identical letters with *no* intervening vowel, we write only one letter. ***Read and write:***

......ممثل......ممثل **mumá<u>thth</u>il** *representative* ......اول......اول **áwwal** *first*

> **Doubled Letter Rule.** *Letters which are sounded double (i.e. with no intervening vowel) are written single.*

Although we write the doubled letter single, it is most important to *pronounce* it doubled, i.e. *hold* it for longer than normal. Imagine saying *butter* as *but-ter*. The two words shown above then sound as if they were transcribed **áw-wal** and **mumá<u>th</u>-<u>th</u>il**. This is the correct pronunciation.

Think of the double *-nn-* in *innumerable*. If you know Italian, you have no problem; think of the double *-tt-* in *città*.

There is a way of showing doubled letters in script. It is the sign called

> ّ **<u>sh</u>ádda**

This sign, which is not a letter of the alphabet, can be written above any letter to show that it is doubled. I say 'can be' as it is often left out; but since **<u>sh</u>ádda** is so useful we shall use it for the rest of this book. You should always write it where appropriate.

Read and write, distinguishing single letters from doubled:

لما **lámma** *when*   لمن **li-man** *whose*

ممثّل **mumá<u>thth</u>il** *representative*   مثل **mi<u>th</u>l** *like*

تلال **tilā́l** *hills*   تلّ **tall** *hill*

Exercise 4 Put **<u>sh</u>adda** wherever appropriate, and pronounce the word. The first one is done:

(a) ممثّل **mumá<u>thth</u>il** (b) تمويل (c) اول (d) ممنون

Give the meaning of each word. The first is *representative.*

The answers to this exercise follow paragraph 5 below.

5 Definite Article - *The*

The important word *the* is called the *definite article*, or more simply the *article*. We use it before a *noun* (i.e. a word denoting a person, place, thing or idea). In Arabic, it takes the form ..ال **al-**, which is always attached to the word which it 'defines', i.e. makes definite. We show it with a hyphen; you should pronounce the whole thing as one word.

Read and write:

البيت **al-bayt** *the house*

البنات **al-banā́t** *the daughters*

The article is used in Arabic more often than is *the* in English; it is especially common with geographical terms, and with words used in a general or universal meaning.

Read and write these examples:

اليابان **al-yābā́n** *('the') Japan*

الموت **al-mowt** *('the') death* (i.e. in general)

al- is its normal pronunciation. But when the defined word begins with a sound pronounced with the tip or near-tip of the tongue, the **l** merges with (the technical term is 'assimilates to') that sound, producing a doubled sound. The spelling stays the same. Look carefully first at the spelling and pronunciation of the following expressions, then ***read and write*** them. We show the doubled letter with **<u>sh</u>ádda**:

........التّل........ التّل **at-tall** (not ***al-***...) *the hill*

........التّلال........ التّلال **at-tilā́l** *the hills*

........النّيل........ النّيل **an-nīl** *the Nile*

........الثّالث........ الثّالث **a<u>th</u>-<u>th</u>ā́li<u>th</u>** *the third one*

........اللون........ اللون* **al-loun** *the colour*

........اللبناني........ اللبناني* **al-lubnā́nī** *the Lebanese (person)*

There are fourteen letters which have this effect on the **l** of the article. So far we have learned four of them: ت , ث , ن and ل . The fourteen letters concerned are called by the Arabs 'sun letters'. We shall point out the remaining ten sun letters as we meet them. The important thing to remember is that in such words we pronounce as double the first letter of the defined word, dropping the **l** of the article in pronunciation but not in spelling.

* Two letters **l** written together, even though there is no intervening vowel. This is an exception to the rule about doubled letters.

You will also have noticed that the article ..ال never affects the stress of the word, and never takes the stress itself.

One final note: the ..ال of الماني *German* is not the article; it is part of the word itself. We learn in Unit 3 how to add the article to a word like this.

Exercise 5 Make each word definite with the article. Write your answer, then match it with the transcription and the meaning. The first one is done:

(a) بيت → البيت **al-bayt** *the house* (b) ممثّل (c) تمويل (d) نبات
an-nabā́t, at-tamwī́l, al-mumá<u>thth</u>il; *(the) financing, the representative, the vegetation.*

Exercise 6 In your answers to Exercise 5, underline the articles whose **l** assimilates to a sun letter at the beginning of the defined word.

Exercise 7 Why are ا , ب , ي , م and و so-called 'moon' letters, i.e. not sun letters? (Pronounce them, and you will see - or rather, feel - why.)

The answers to these exercises are immediately below.

Answers to Exercises

Exercise 1 (b) **تمام tamā́m** *perfect* (c) **ثالث <u>th</u>ā́li<u>th</u>** *third* (d) **ثلاث <u>th</u>alā́<u>th</u>** *three*

Exercise 2 (a) ثلاث (b) آلات (c) لا

Exercise 3 (a) **الماني almā́nī** *German* (b) **ياباني yābā́nī** *Japanese* (c) **لبناني lubnā́nī** *Lebanese* (d) **ليبي lī́bī** *Libyan*

Exercise 4 (a) **ممثّل mumá<u>thth</u>il** *representative* (b) **تمويل tamwī́l** *financing,* (c) **اوّل áwwal** *first,* (d) **ممنون mamnū́n** *grateful*

Exercise 5 (b) **الممثّل al-mumá<u>thth</u>il** *the representative* (b) **التمويل at-tamwī́l** *(the) financing* (d) **النّبات an-nabā́t** *the vegetation*

Exercise 6 (c) <u>الـ</u>تّمويل (d) <u>الـ</u>نّبات

Exercise 7 Because they are not pronounced with the tip or near-tip of the tongue.

Tests

1 Write the letters as a word. For example, (a) ال ن ي ل is النّيل :

(a) ال ن ي ل (b) ال ت م و ي ل (c) ا و و ل

(d) ال م ا ن ي (e) م م ن و ن

2 Read aloud your handwritten answers to Test 1. For example, (a) is **an-nīl.**

3 Read aloud. For example, (a) is **lubnā́nī**:

(a) لبناني (b) اوّل (c) الثالث

(d) ممنون (e) النمل

4 Write. For example, (a) is الليبي :

(a) **al-lī́bī** (b) **muma<u>thth</u>iláyn** (c) **at-tamwī́l**
(d) **an-nīláyn*** (e) **ow** (f) **al-yābā́nī**
(* i.e. two, the Blue and the White. They meet at Khartoum.)

5 In the following list, the words ابن\البنات\اب form a group as they all denote family relationships. Assemble the other logical groups, and say why their words belong together:

ابن، الماني، الثالث، البنات، يونيو، البيوت، اب، اول،
ياباني، لبناني، يوليو، البنايات، اثنين، ثلاث، آب، ليبي،
مايو.

Review

In this Unit we studied three common letters and one special sign called **<u>sh</u>ádda**. You learned also

- how to read and write the special forms of **lām-álif**,
- how to join the letter **mīm**,
- how to write doubled letters,
- how to express the article *the*, and how to pronounce it,

You have had more practice with tall, shallow and deep shapes.

Hopefully you have also become a little more fluent in reading and writing, and you probably now find writing ‘the other way round’ less strange.

3

In this unit you will learn

- a very important non-alphabetical sign,
- more about the article *the*,
- three more letters, plus one variant, with their pronunciation,
- more words,
- how to make 'feminine' words.

hámza

1 Listen to someone say emphatically: 'absolutely awful'. You will hear a catch of the breath before each of the *a*'s. We could represent it with an apostrophe: *'absolutely 'awful.*

This is called a 'glottal stop', the glottis being that part of the throat which stops or releases breath when we speak. The stop is written in Arabic with a non-alphabetical sign called **hámza**:

ء **hámza**

hámza is never joined to anything. Write it several times:

............ء ....ء ....ء ....ء ....ء

............ء............ء............ء............ء............ء

Its form is simple enough, but it is used in many ways. You will see it in the following guises:

- above or below **álif**: أ إ ,
- above **wow**, or **yā** *without its dots*: ؤ ئ ئ ,
- standing alone, on or near the line of writing: ء .

Whole chapters have been written about the correct writing of **hámza**. For our purposes, it is sufficient if we learn to pronounce the glottal stop whenever we see the sign ء. We transcribe it with an apostrophe: ' .

Many Arabic words apparently beginning with a vowel, such as **ab**, in fact begin with a glottal stop. The writing often marks it with **hámza**, but it is equally often ignored.

For clarity, from now on in this book we shall show initial **hámza** on the Arabic of all words which have it, thus: أب . We shall continue to transcribe without the apostrophe.

You should continue to write without initial **hámza**; that is always acceptable.

In the middle or at the end of a word, however, the **hámza** is always written, and you should write it, too.

One last point: آ **álif mádda** is deemed to have an 'in-built' **hámza**, so while the stop is pronounced, no 'further' **hámza** is written.

Read and write:

انباء .... أنباء **anbā'** *news (items)* .... نبأ نبأ **nába'** *news item*

نائم .... نائم **nā'im** *asleep* .... الآن الآن **'al-'ān** *now*

تنبّؤ .... تنبّؤ **tanábbu'** *forecast* .... ثنائي ثنائي **thunā'ī** *double*

Definite Article (continued)

2 In Unit 2 we learned the article ..الـ: البيت, النيل.

When we attach the article to a word beginning with **hámza**, the **hámza** has to be written (unless we have **álif mádda**, in which the **hámza** is already present). We can leave out the **hámza** at the beginning of a word, but not once an article is added, since the **hámza** is now in the middle of the word. The article itself has no **hámza.**

Read and write:

الأب .... الأب **al-'ab** *the father* .... اب أب *father*

الإبل .... الإبل **al-'ibil** *the camels* .... ابل إبل *camels*

الأنباء .... الأنباء **al-'anbā'** *the news items* .... انباء أنباء *news items*

الآلات .... الآلات **al-'ālāt** *the tools* .... آلات آلات *tools*

Some words begin with vowels which are deemed to have no stop, i.e. no **hámza**. ***Read and write*** the two already known to us:

........الابن........ الابن **al-ibn** *the son* ....ابن........ ابن *son*

........الاثنين........ الاثنين **al-ithnayn** *the two* ....اثنين........ اثنين *two*

Words of one letter

3 A few important words consist of one letter. ***Read and write:***

....ل... ل **li** *to, for* .....ب.... ب **bi** *with, by, in* ....و... و **wa** *and*

It is a rule that one-letter words are written as part of the next word, e.g.:

............لبنات... لبنات **li-banāt** *for girls* ......وأنا... وأنا **wa-'ána** *and I*

which we transcribe with a hyphen for clarity. The article ..الـ itself does not begin with a **hámza** but with a so-called 'weak' vowel, that is, a vowel which is dropped when another vowel precedes it. This happens when a one-letter word is added to the article.

Read and write:

............باليابان........ باليابان **bi-l-yāban** (not ***bi-al-***) *in Japan*

............والنّيل........ والنّيل **wa-n-nīl** *and the Nile*

When the word ل (see above) is added to the article, the **álif** of the article is dropped in writing too:

............للبنات........ للبنات **li-l-banāt** *to/for (the) girls*

............للتّمويل........ للتّمويل **li-t-tamwīl** *for (the) financing*

We do not, however, write more than two consecutive identical letters, even when the expression seems to demand more. Read and write:

............للّبناني........ للّبناني **li-l-lubnānī** *for the Lebanese (man)*

Exercise 1 Write these words with the definite article, and pronounce them:

(a) ألماني (b) إبل (c) أنباء (d) أب (e) أول

Fit the meanings to your answers: *the first, the news, the camels, the German, the father.*

Exercise 2 Add لِ to your answers to Exercise 1 in writing. Give the meaning. Then fit the pronunciation to your answers:

li-l-'anbā́', li-l-'ab, li-l-'almā́nī, li-l-'ā́wwal, li-l-'ibil.

The answers to these exercises follow paragraph 6 below.

Letters

4

ه	ـه	ـه	ـهـ	ـهـ	هـ	**hā**

By far the most complicated letter in this alphabet, **hā** represents the sound *h* (as in English *he*). The **h** is sounded wherever you see the letter, even at the end of a word, unlike English. **hā** is a joined letter, shallow except in one case, with several possible forms:

- هـ at the beginning of a word or after a disjoined letter,
- *ـهـ or ـهـ in the middle of a word after a joined letter,
- ـه or *ـه at the end of a word after a joined letter,
- ه at the end of a word after a disjoined letter, or when standing alone.

* The middle form ـهـ is little used in handwriting, and the final form ـه is not used in print or typing.

Let us take this letter in stages. Everything rests on the line of writing except for the downward tick of ـهـ. Write first several initial letters **hā**:

Now the handwritten middle form:

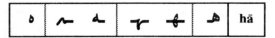

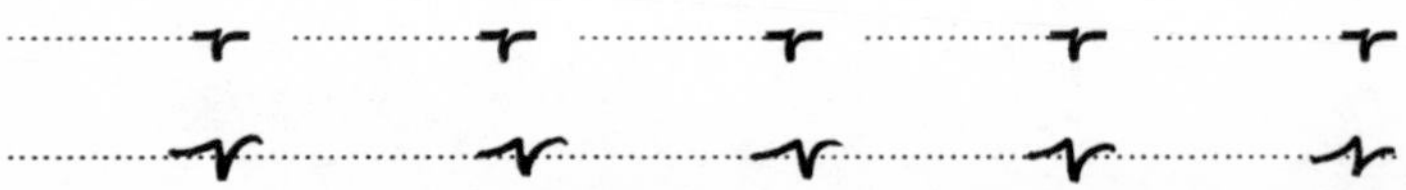

Then the two final forms, both used in handwriting:

............ـه ....ـه ....ـه ....ـه ....ـه

............ـه ....ـه ....ـه ....ـه ....ـه

And finally the 'isolated' form:

............ه ....ه ....ه ....ه ....ه

............ه ....ه ....ه ....ه ....ه

Now ***read and write:***

......هي...... هي **híya** *she* ......هو...... هو **húwa** *he*

......هامّ...... هامّ **hāmm** *important* ......هم...... هم **hum** *they*

......اهتمام...... اهتمام **ihtimā́m** *attention* ......نهائي...... نهائي **nihā́'ī** *final*

......تنبيه...... تنبيه **tanbī́h** *warning* ......انتباه...... انتباه **intibā́h** *caution*

......تمهّل...... تمهّل **tamáhhal** *SLOW DOWN (road sign)*

One important word with **hā** is spelt irregularly. Note: **الله allā́h** *God*.

5

ة ـة ـة tā marbū́ṭa

This one is a 'curiosity'. It is not an alphabetical letter, but final **hā** with the two dots of **tā**, and it is called **tā marbū́ṭa***, which means 'bound **tā**'. It is found only at the end of words, and is commonly used to make certain words 'feminine'. After a consonant, it has the sound **-a**; combined with **ـي ī** it gives the combination **...ـية -ī́ya**. In handwriting the dots of **ة** are frequently left off; in print, never.

* The name of this letter itself contains a letter (**ṭ**) which we have not yet studied. No panic. We shall learn it properly the next time it occurs.

Read and write, comparing the 'masculine' ('m.') and 'feminine' ('f.') forms of words known to you:

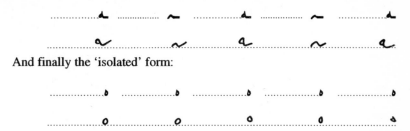

grateful:	........ممنون........	ممنون	(m., of a man or boy)			
	........ممنونة........	ممنونة	**mamnū́na** (f., of a woman or girl)			
important:	........هامّة........	هامّة	**hā́mma** (f.)	........هامّ........	هامّ	(m.)
third:	........ثالثة........	ثالثة	**<u>th</u>ā́li<u>th</u>a** (f.)	........ثالث........	ثالث	(m.)
Japanese:	........يابانية........	يابانية	**yābānī́ya** (f.)	........ياباني........	ياباني	(m.)
German:	........ألمانية........	ألمانية	**almānī́ya** (f.)	........ألماني........	ألماني	(m.)
Lebanese:	........لبنانية........	لبنانية	**lubnānī́ya** (f.)	........لبناني........	لبناني	(m.)

The ending **-ī́ya** carries the stress of the word, as shown.

Exercise 3 Match these words with their sound and their meaning given in the list below. The first one is done for you:

(a) ثنائي **<u>th</u>una'ī** *double* (b) ممنونة (c) ليبية (d) اهتمام

mamnū́na, **ihtimā́m**, **lībī́ya**; *attention, grateful, Libyan.*

Exercise 4 Complete the word with the right handwritten form of **hā**:

(a) نـ..ائي (b) ...و (c) انتبا... (d) ...امّ (e) ...ي

Read your answers aloud.

Exercise 5 Feminine (f.) or masculine (m.)?:

(a) ألماني (b) ممنونة (c) هي (d) هامّ (e) لبنانية

Read each word aloud.

The answers to these exercises follow paragraph 6 below.

6

ســ س	**sīn**
شــ ش	**<u>sh</u>īn**

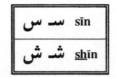

The letters called **sīn** and **<u>sh</u>īn** represent the sounds *s* (as in English *see*) and *<u>sh</u>* (as in English *she*) respectively. These are joined letters; the short and full forms are used like the short and full forms of ب . Short-form **sīn** and **<u>sh</u>īn** are shallow and rest on the line of writing. The full form has a deep swoop. The two letters differ only in the dots, which are always situated as shown.

Despite appearances, these are not toothed letters (Unit 1, paragraph 6). In handwriting, we usually 'iron out' the indentations of these letters into a shallow curve, thus: ﺳ   ﺳ

Write several examples of each letter, first with indentations and printed dots, then with a curve and the dots run together into a circumflex (see Unit 1, paragraph 3):

sīn and s̲h̲īn are sun letters, so the ل of the article assimilates: as-, as̲h̲-.

Read and write:

السّنة الـــنه   as-sana *the year*   سنة سنـه   sana *year*

الاسم الاسم   al-ism *the name*   اسم اسم   ism *name*

الأساس الأساس   al-'asās *the basis*   أساس اساس   asās *basis*

شاي شاي   s̲h̲āy *tea*   شيء شيء   s̲h̲ay' *thing*

الشّمس الشّمس   as̲h̲-s̲h̲ams *the sun*   شمس شمس   s̲h̲ams *sun*

شمالي شمالي   s̲h̲imālī *northern*   شمال شمال   s̲h̲imāl *north*

سؤال سؤال   su'āl *question*   مسؤول مسؤول   mas'ūl *responsible*

تأسيس تأسيس   ta'sīs *foundation* (the action)

التأسيس التأسيس   at-ta'sīs *the foundation*

ملابس ملابس   malābis *clothes*

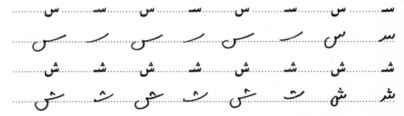

Exercise 6 Read aloud the following signs and announcements:

(c)

(b)

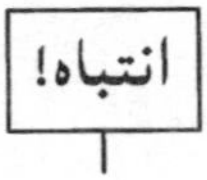

(a)

(d)

What do they mean?

The answers to this exercise are immediately below.

Answers to Exercises

Exercise 1 (a) **الألماني al-'almā́nī** *the German*
(b) **الإبل al-'íbil** *the camels* (c) **الأنباء al-'anbā́'** *the news*
(d) **الأب al-'ab** *the father* (e) **الأوّل al-'áwwal** *the first*

Exercise 2 (a) **للألماني li-l-'almā́nī** *for the German*
(b) **للإبل li-l-'íbil** *for the camels* (c) **للأنباء li-l-'anbā́'** *for the news*
(d) **للأب li-l-'ab** *for the father* (e) **للأوّل li-l-'áwwal** *for the first*

Exercise 3 (b) **mamnū́na** *grateful* (c) **lībī́ya** *Libyan*
(d) **ihtimā́m** *attention*

Exercise 4 (a) **نهائي nihā́'ī** (b) **هو húwa** (c) **انتباه intibāh**
(d) **هامّ hāmm** (e) **هي híya**

Exercise 5 (a) **almā́nī** m. (b) **mamnū́na** f. (c) **híya** f. (d) **hāmm** m.
(e) **lubnānī́ya** f.

Exercise 6 (a) **bayt bi-l-'a<u>th</u>ā́<u>th</u>** *House with Furniture*
(b) **intibā́h!** *CAUTION!* (c) **malā́bis li-l-banā́t** *Clothes for Girls*
(d) **tamáhhal** *SLOW DOWN*

Tests

1 Write the letters as a word. For example, (a) ش م س is شمس :

(a) ش م س (b) ال ا س م (c) ال م م ث ث ل
(d) أ ن ب ا ء (e) ث ن ا ء ي

2 Read aloud your handwritten answers to Test 1. For example, (a) is shams.

3 Read aloud. For example, (a) is **al-ihtimám**:

(a) الاهتمام (b) اللبنانية (c) الألمانية
(d) بالأوّل (e) بالثالثة

4 Put into the masculine form. For example, (a) is ممنون :

(a) ممنونة (b) يابانية (c) اللبنانية
(d) مسؤولة (e) للثالثة

5 Pronounce your answers to Test 4. For example, (a) is **mamnún**.

6 In the last three units you have read and written all the following words. Fill in the missing letter in each one, in the right form. The first is نـ , making لبنانية:

(a) لبـ..انية (b) ا...تمام (c) الملابـ..
(d) البـ..وت (e) ثانـ..ـي

If you have difficulty, you will find word (a) in paragraph 5 above, (b) in paragraph 4 above, (c) in paragraph 6 above (without its article), and (d) and (e) in Unit 2, paragraph 3.

Review

In this unit we studied three common letters, one variant, and the important sign called **hámza**. We also finished the article **al-** and its variants; you can now make definite any noun you know.

In this unit you also learned about feminine words and one-letter words. Your vocabulary now begins to expand spontaneously.

Finally, you have read four signs with authentic Arabic wording, using your knowledge under 'field' conditions.

4

In this unit you will learn

- six more letters, all of them sun letters,
- about 'dark' sounds,
- how to make common 'relative' words.

Letters

1

ر	**rā**
ز	**zayy**

The letters called **rā** and **zayy** represent respectively *r* (which is always *rolled*, wherever it occurs) and *z* as in English *zoo*. These are *sun* letters, and are *disjoined*. The only difference in their appearance is the dot on **zayy**.

They are deep letters, written just like و **wow**, but without the ring, i.e. they start just above or at the line of writing, and make a half-swoop down and a little leftwards, but not up again. Write several:

ر........ز........ر........ز........ر........ز..........

ر........ز........ر........ز........ر........ز..........

These letters are joined to the previous letter in the normal way, except that, in handwriting, when they follow a tooth which is itself preceded by a letter, they have a special connection. Write the handwritten forms for **rā** (**zayy** is exactly the same, with a dot), paying special attention to the connection:

tooth + *tooth* + **r**	ببر ...... ببر......
m + *tooth* + **r**	مبر ...... مبر......
l + *tooth* + *r*	لبر ...... لبر......
s + *tooth* + **r**	سبر ...... سبر......

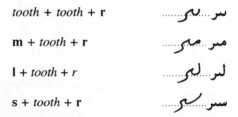

The short vowel **a** and the long vowel **ā**, when next to **rā**, are almost always 'darkened' in sound; the **a** sounds more like *u* in Southern English *but*, and the **ā** sounds more like the *a* of English *calm*. You will certainly notice it when you hear Arabs speak. Imitate it if you can; it is however not wrong or unintelligible if you don't.

In the list given below, 'dark' **a** and **ā** are shown as **ạ** and **ạ̄**, to help you.

Read and write:

مسرور	**masrū́r** *pleased*	مرور	**murū́r** *traffic*
متر	**mitr** *metre*	مرّة	**mạ́rrạ** *a time*
ليرة	**lī́rạ** *lira*	لتر	**litr** *litre*
الرّيال	**ạr-riyā́l**	ريال	**riyā́l** *rial, riyal*
الرّئيس	**ạr-rạ'ī́s**	رئيس	**rạ'ī́s** *chairman**
الزّيارة	**az-ziyạ̄́rạ**	زيارة	**ziyạ̄́rạ** *visit*
شهر	**shahr** *month*	إيران	**īrạ̄́n** *Iran*
سيّارة	**sayyạ̄́rạ** *car*	وزارة	**wizạ̄́rạ** *ministry*

* also *chief, president, head* (person)

2

د	**dāl**
ذ	**<u>dh</u>āl**

These two letters, called **dāl** and **<u>dh</u>āl**, represent respectively *d* as in English *day* and hard *th* as in English *that*. Don't confuse this last sound with the soft *th* of **ث <u>th</u>ā** (*think*), for which see Unit 1, paragraph 3.

These are both sun letters, and are disjoined. The only difference in their appearance is the dot on **<u>dh</u>āl**.

At first it seems they might be confused with **rā** and **zayy**. But there are important differences: **ذ د** are shallow, resting on the line of writing, and are always joined at the 'elbow'; ز ر are deep, and always joined at the head. Write several examples of **dāl** and **dhāl**:

.... ذ .... د .... ذ .... د .... ذ .... د

.... ذ ذ د ذ د ذ د

Read and write:

إدارة .... إدارة idára *administration*   الإدارة al-'idára

دراسة .... دراسة dirása *study*   الدّراسة ad-dirása

دائرة .... دائرة dá'ira *directorate*   الدائرة ad-dá'ira

مدرسة .... مدرسة mádrasa *school*   مدير .... مدير mudír *director*

أستاذ .... أستاذ ustádh *professor*   الأستاذ al-'ustádh

ابتداء .... ابتداء ibtidá' *beginning*   الابتداء al-ibtidá'

سيّد .... سيّد sayyid *gentleman; Mr*   سيّدة .... sayyida *lady; Mrs*

Exercise 1 Whose are these office doors? Read out their titles in Arabic and English:

(d) الأستاذ   (c) الممثّل   (b) الرئيس   (a) المدير

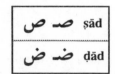

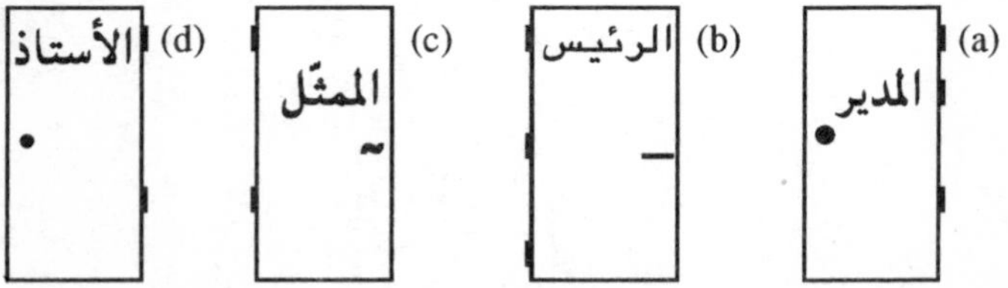

The answers to this exercise follow paragraph 4 below.

3

ص ـص	şād
ض ـض	ḍād

Dark sounds

These two letters represent 'dark' sounds.

Think of the familiar sound *s*, represented by س **sīn** (Unit 3). In pronouncing it, the tongue is high, following the curve of the palate. Now say *s* again, but this time dropping your tongue as low as possible, making a cavity at the bottom of the mouth. The *s* which you pronounce in this manner is 'dark'. It is ṣ, which is the sound of the letter **ṣād**.

Similarly, **ḍ** is a *d* said with low tongue, forming a cavity. It is the dark equivalent of the more familiar **d** of د **dāl** (paragraph 2 above).

An immortal Australian writer once said his countrymen enjoy 'sin in the sun'. Think of the two *s*'s in this phrase, and the idea of light and dark letters seems less strange.

So much for the sounds. As to the shapes, **ṣād** and **ḍād** are both written identically except for the dot. They are joined, sun letters. The short form is shallow, resting on the line. Also, immediately after the loop it has a built-in tooth, which is never left out. The full form is deep, with a swoop. Write several:

صـ .... ص .... ضـ .... ض .... صـ .... ص .... ضـ .... ض ....

صـ .... ص .... ضـ .... ض .... صـ .... ص .... ضـ .... ض ....

Because of the tooth of short-form **ṣād/ḍād**, there are special connections in handwriting for **ṣ/ḍ + m** and **ṣ/ḍ + r**. Write the combinations (with **ṣ**; those with **ḍ** are identical in outline):

ṣ + m: .... صمـ صم .... صمـ صم   **ṣ + r**: .... صر .... صر

In pronunciation, these letters 'darken' any adjacent **a** or **ā** just as ر **rā** does (paragraph 1 above). In the list below, dark **a** and **ā** are identified with a dot. ***Read and write:***

.... الصوت الصّوت	**aṣ-ṣowt**	.... صوت صوت	**ṣowt** *voice*
.... باص باص	**bāṣ** *bus*	.... وصول وصول	**wuṣūl** *arrival*
.... ضروره ضرورة	**ḍarūra** *necessity*	.... مصر مصر	**miṣr** Egypt
.... اضراب إضراب	**iḍrāb** *strike*	.... مريض مريض	**mariḍ** *sick* (m.)

Relatives

4 You will have noticed a connection between such words as لبنان
Lebanon and لبناني *Lebanese*.

The first word of the pair is a *noun*, i.e. a word denoting a person, place,
thing or idea (in this case, a place). The second word is either another
noun or an *adjective*, i.e. a word describing a noun. We call this kind of
word a 'relative'. In English we have many ways of making relatives,
but Arabic uses mostly one device, i.e. adding ...ي to the base noun.

There are two simple rules for adding the relative ending ...ي :

■ the base noun must be in its indefinite form,

■ the ending can be added only to a consonant, so we must remove
any final vowel (usually a final ا **álif** or a ة **tā marbúṭa**) from the
base noun.

Applying the first rule, we can derive the relative ياباني *Japanese* from
اليابان *Japan*, taking care first to remove the article from the base noun,
to make it indefinite.

Applying the second rule, we can make ضرورة *necessity* (see the list
immediately above) into the relative ضروري **ḍarúrī** *necessary*; and
similarly with countless other nouns ending in a vowel which we remove
before adding the relative ending.

Read and write these nouns, most of which you know, and their
relatives:

الألماني الماني	ألماني	الألمانيا الأ لما نيا	al-'almániya *Germany*
ليبي ليبي	ليبي	ليبيا * ليبيا	líbiya *Libya*
لبناني لبناني	لبناني	لبنان لبنان	
ياباني يابا ني	ياباني	اليابان اليابان	
سوري سوري	سوري **súrī**	سوريا سوريا	súriya *Syria*
إيراني إيراني	إيراني *Iranian*	إيران إيران	
ضروري ضروري	ضروري	ضرورة ضروره	

أساسي	*basic*	أساس
رئيسي	*main, principal*	رئيس
دراسي	*academic*	دراسة
مصري	*Egyptian*	مصر
ابتدائي	*primary, initial*	ابتداء

These relatives are in their masculine form, and indefinite. We know from earlier in this book that we can make such words definite (الياباني), or feminine (يابانية), or definite feminine (اليابانية).

* ليبيا is probably the only word of more than one letter in the Arabic language that reads the same backwards as forwards. Try it.

Exercise 2 Make the masculine relative from each of these nouns. Translate your answers:

(a) أساس (b) مصر (c) إدارة (d) ابتداء (e) وزارة

Exercise 3 Make these relatives definite feminine:

(a) مصري (b) سوري (c) إيراني (d) إسرائيلي*

* **isrā'īlī** in the masculine. Guess its meaning.

Exercise 4 Transcribe these words, marking with a dot the dark **a**'s and **ā**'s. Why are they dark?

(a) ضرورة (b) مريض (c) دراسة (d) الباص (e) ملابس

The answers to these exercises are immediately below.

Answers to Exercises

Exercise 1 (a) **al-mudīr** *Director* (b) **ar-ra'īs** *Chairman* (c) **al-mumáththil** *Representative* (d) **al-'ustādh** *Professor*

Exercise 2 (a) أساسي *basic* (b) مصري *Egyptian* (c) إداري *administrative* (d) ابتدائي *primary, initial* (e) وزاري *ministerial*

Exercise 3 (a) المصرية (b) السورية (c) الإيرانية (d) الإسرائيلية

Exercise 4 (a) **ḍarū́rạ**, two **a**'s next to **r**, one next to **ḍ** (b) **mạrī́ḍ**, **a** next to **r** (c) **dirā́sa**, first **a** next to **r** (d) **al-bāṣ**, **ā** next to **ṣ** (e) none

Tests

1 Write, paying attention to special connections:

(a) مصرية (b) اهتمام (c) تمام
(d) ضروري (e) ألماني

2 Read aloud your handwritten answers to Test 1.

3 Read aloud:

(a) الإيرانية (b) مريض (c) للسورية
(d) ابتدائي (e) بالألمانيا

4 Give the base word from which the relative is derived. Translate the base word and the relative:

(a) أساسي (b) دراسي (c) إداري
(d) لليبية (e) الإسرائيلية

5 Pronounce your answers to Test 4. For example, (a) is **asā́s**.

6 Fill in the missing letter in each word:

(a) الـ..صرية (b) إد...رة (c) مد...ر
(d) الشـ...ء (e) مريـ..ة

Review

In this unit we studied six more letters, including the last four disjoined ones and a pair with 'dark' sounds. You also learned how to derive 'relatives'. This is a big step forward, as there are hundreds of such derived words. You can say that you have added about 10% to your vocabulary at one stroke.

Keep writing. Perhaps your main objective in following this book is to learn how to read; but it is writing which will fix things in your memory.

We have done most of the alphabetical section of this book. There are ten letters to go, all of them in groups or pairs like most of the others; and three more 'curiosities'.

You will have noticed that, because some letters have alternative forms or special connections, you have to think ahead as you write. That gets easier when you begin to see the whole word in your mind; and that comes with practice.

5

In this unit you will learn

- seven more letters, with their pronunciation,
- when and how to join these letters,
- words which you can read and write using the seven letters,
- more about *stress*.

Letters

1

ج	جـ	**jīm**
ح	حـ	**ḥā**
خ	خـ	**<u>kh</u>ā**

A family of joined letters, each with a short and full form used exactly like those of ب . The only difference between these three is the dot.

ج **jīm** sounds like *j* in English *jam* in most Arab countries. In Egypt it sounds like hard *g* in English *go*. We use the sound *j* in this book.

ح **ḥā** is a heavy *h*; it is the sound made when we breathe on glass to clean it. To an Arab it sounds quite distinct from ه **hā**, which we learned in Unit 3. Try to make the distinction yourself.

خ **<u>kh</u>ā** represents the sound of *ch* in Scottish *loch* or Welsh *bach*.

The short forms are shallow, resting on the line of writing. The full forms are deep, with a *reverse* half-swoop, the head still resting on the line.

Read and write a line of each letter, starting at its top left-hand corner:

جـ ج جـ ج جـ ج

جـ ج جـ ج جـ ج

حـ ح حـ ح حـ ح

حـ ح حـ ح حـ ح

خـ خ خـ خ خـ خ

خـ خ خـ خ خـ خ

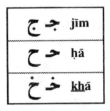

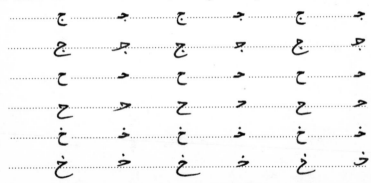

An **a** or **ā** next to خ is often (not always) pronounced dark. Imitate what you hear. Don't be confused by the transcription of ح **ḥā**; it is *not* a dark letter. We transcribe it in this manner merely to distinguish it from ه **hā**.

Read and write a few new words:

جنوبي جنوبي **janūbī** *southern* جنوب جنوب **janū́b** *south*

دخول دخول **dukhū́l** *entry** خروج خروج **khurū́j** *exit**

* the *action*. The *place* is **mákhraj** or **mádkhal**, see below.

When one of these letters is joined to a previous joined letter in print, the connection is often at the right-hand corner of the ج etc.; in handwriting we make the connection at the beginning of the outline, i.e. the left-hand corner. Compare print with handwriting below (for ج only; the others go the same way); practise the handwritten forms:

	handwriting	*print*
tooth + **j**	بج بجـ	بج بجـ\بجـ
teeth + **j**	سج سجـ	سج سجـ
l + j	لج لجـ	لج لجـ\لجـ
m + j	مج مجـ	مج مجـ
s + j	سج سجـ	سج سجـ

(and so on, with other preceding joined letters)

Read and write:

لجنة لجنة **lájna** *committee* احتجاج احتجاج **iḥtijāj** *objection*

أجنبي اجنبي **ájnabī** *foreign* إنتاج انتاج **intā́j** *production*

مدخل مدخل **mádkhal** *entrance* مخرج مخرج **mákhraj** *exit*

انتخاب انتخاب **intikhā́b** *election* أخبار اخبار **akhbā́r** *news*

خاصّ خاصّ **khāṣṣ** *private, special, particular*

2

ط	ṭā
ظ	ẓā

The letters called **ṭā** and **ẓā** are joined letters, yet they have only one form each. It is tall, and always rests on the line. Despite the similarity with ص (Unit 4, paragraph 3), the loop of these letters has no tooth-like projection after it, as does ص. Write a line of these letters, first the loop, then the upright:

ط ...... ظ ...... ط ...... ظ ...... ط ...... ظ ......

ط ...... ظ ...... ط ...... ظ ...... ط ...... ظ ......

These are sun letters with dark sounds. Just as ص is the dark equivalent (tongue low, with cavity) of س , so ط is the dark equivalent of ت , and ظ is the dark equivalent of ز . We transcribe ط with ṭ, and ظ with ẓ. As you might guess, any neighbouring **a** or **ā** is darkened. In the list given below, we dot these two vowels for clarity. ***Read and write:***

طائرة **ṭạ́'irạ** *aeroplane* ...... طائره

مطار **maṭạ̄r** *airport* ...... مطار

وطن **wạ́ṭạn** *nation* ...... وطن

وطني **wạ́ṭạnī** *national* ...... وطني

شرطة **shúrṭạ** *police* ...... شرطه

خطّ **khạṭṭ** *line* ...... خطّ

بريطانيا **bạrīṭạ̄niya** *Britain* ...... بريطانيا

إيطاليا **īṭạ̄liya** *Italy* ...... ايطاليا

خطر **khạ́ṭạr** *danger*, **khạṭir** *dangerous* ...... خطر

تنظيم **tanẓīm** *organisation* (the activity) ...... تنظيم

منظّمة **munạ́ẓẓạma** *organisation* (the body) ...... منظّمه

Exercise 1 Read the following signs:

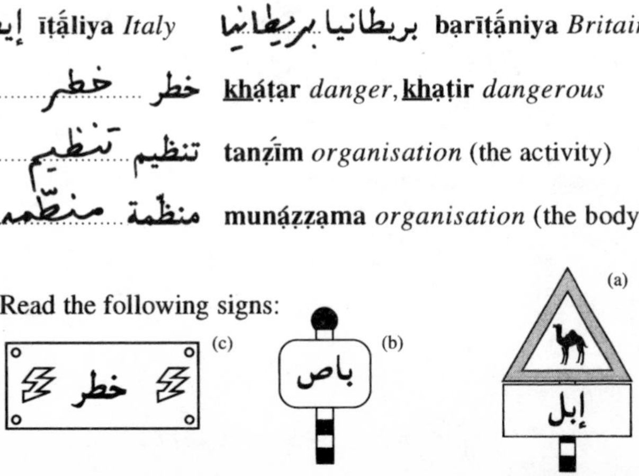

Exercise 2 Fill in the missing letter:

(a) إ...تاج (b) و...ني (c) انتـ..اب (d) ابتـ..ائي (e) منـ..مة

Exercise 3 List at least twelve nouns beginning with a sun letter, and at least twelve nouns beginning with another (i.e. a 'moon') letter. Make them all definite with the article. Read your answers aloud, and translate them.

Exercise 4 Write, in the masculine singular, all the words you can remember denoting a nationality. Now write all the words you can remember denoting a profession or function. Read everything aloud and translate.

The answers to Exercises 1 and 2 follow paragraph 4.

3

ع	ـع	ـعـ	عـ	**9ayn**
غ	ـغ	ـغـ	غـ	**ghayn**

Here comes probably the most difficult sound in the Arabic language. It is the sound of the letter **9ayn**, which we transcribe with **9**, since no letter in our alphabet comes anywhere near its sound. Say to yourself the name *Maggie*. Keep repeating it, but as you do so, try to stop making contact in your throat for the *-gg-* in the middle, i.e. let the middle consonant become more and more vague until it feels no more than a gulp. You are probably saying something like معي **má9ī** *with me*. Now do it again, but get to the target sound faster. Say it again and again until you can hit it first time, without Maggie's help. The correct sound is a little like the name *Marie* as pronounced in French, but without the contact of the French *r*.

The sound of the other letter, which we transcribe as **gh**, is the 'hard' equivalent of **kh**, for which see paragraph 1 above. It sounds somewhat like the French *r* of *Marie*, but shorter.

ع and غ are joined letters. The two short forms rest on the line, and the two full forms have a reverse half-swoop like ج. The different forms are used as follows:

- عـ and غـ are written at the beginning of a word, or in the middle of a word after a *disjoined* letter,
- ـعـ and ـغـ are written in the middle of a word after a *joined* letter,
- ـع and ـغ are written at the end of a word after a *joined* letter,
- ع and غ are written at the end of a word after a *disjoined* letter, or when standing alone.

Or we can put it far more simply: the 'solid' forms stand after a joined letter, and the 'open' forms stand everywhere else.

Write several of each:

........غـ........عـ........غـ........عـ........غـ........عـ

........غـ........عـ........غـ........عـ........غـ........عـ

........ـغـ........ـعـ........ـغـ........ـعـ........ـغـ........ـعـ

........ـغـ........ـعـ........ـغـ........ـعـ........ـغـ........ـعـ

........ـغ........ـع........ـغ........ـع........ـغ........ـع

........ـغ........ـع........ـغ........ـع........ـغ........ـع

........غ........ع........غ........ع........غ........ع

........غ........ع........غ........ع........غ........ع

Read and write:

........سعر سعر	**si9r** *price*	........عامّ عامّ	**9āmm** *general, public*
........مطعم مطعم	**máṭ9am** *restaurant*	........صناعة صناعة	**ṣiná̄9a** *industry*
........معلّم معلّم	**mu9állim** *teacher*	........أسبوع أسبوع	**usbú̄9** *week*
........شارع شارع	**<u>sh</u>ā́ri9** *street*	........اجتماع اجتماع	**ijtimá̄9** *meeting*
........غربي غربي	**<u>gh</u>árbī** *western*	........غرب غرب	**<u>gh</u>arb** *west*
........مشغول مشغول	**ma<u>shgh</u>ū́l** *busy*	........مبلغ مبلغ	**máblag<u>h</u>** *sum*

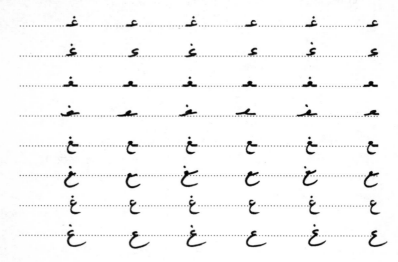

Stress

4 So far we have marked the stress (see Unit 1, paragraph 4) with an accent. But Arabic stress is almost entirely regular, and we can learn and apply simple rules:

- the stress falls on the last so-called 'heavy' syllable if there is one. A 'heavy' syllable is one with either
  - a long vowel (**ā, ī, ū**) or a vowel-combination (**ay, ou, ow**) followed by a consonant (**b, j, d** etc.): **bināýā́t, marī́ḍ, usbū́9, bintáyn,**
  - or a short vowel (**a, i, u**) followed by two consonants* or a doubled consonant: **máblagh, mumáththil,**

    * Remember that consonants transcribed with underlining (**th**, **gh** etc.) are single consonants in Arabic.
- if there is no heavy syllable, the first syllable is stressed: **ána.**

The following elements are never stressed, and are not counted when placing the stress:

- the article **al-, at-** (etc.),
- any vowel (long or short) or vowel-combination ending a word, i.e. with no following consonant. Note that **hámza**, although not an alphabetical letter, counts as a consonant, so that a word like **ibtidā́'** does not end in a vowel; its final syllable counts as heavy, and is herefore stressed. The relative of this word has the same stress (**ibtidā́'ī**).

Now that we have the rules, we no longer need to mark the stress in the transcription.

Exercise 5 Read the signs:

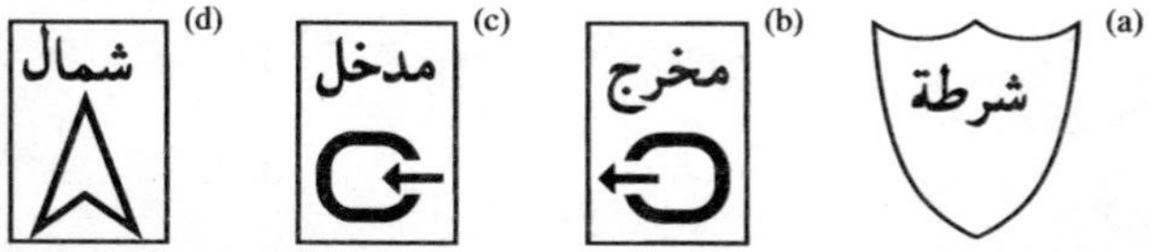

Exercise 6 Mark the stress with an accent on these transcribed words or word-forms which we have not yet studied:

(a) **mashghūlīn** (b) **maḥaṭṭa** (c) **intikhābāt** (d) **tarbiya**

Exercise 7 Complete the word with the right form of ع or غ:

(a) اجتما... (b) مشـ..ـول (c) مـ..ـلّمة (d) مبلـ... (e) ...امّ

Exercise 8 Write in Arabic (putting any relatives or other adjectives in the m. form), and pronounce your answers, taking care with the stress:
(a) *the meeting* (b) *daily* (c) *monthly* (d) *arrival* (e) *south*
(f) *the week* (g) *electoral* (h) *the school* (j) *Italian* (k) *administrative*

Exercise 9 Reading. Covering everything but the printed Arabic, read again, column by column, the 'Read and write' paragraphs of this unit.

The answers to Exercises 5 to 8 are immediately below.

Answers to Exercises

Exercise 1 (a) **íbil** *CAMELS** (b) **bāṣ** *BUS* (c) **kháṭar** *DANGER*

Exercise 2 (a) إنتاج (b) وطني (c) انتخاب (d) ابتدائي (e) منظّمة

Exercise 5 (a) **shurṭa** (b) **makhraj** (c) **madkhal** (d) **shimāl**

Exercise 6 (a) **mashghūlīn** (b) **maḥáṭṭa** (c) **intikhābāt** (d) **tárbiya**

Exercise 7 (a) اجتماع (b) مشغول (c) معلّمة (d) مبلغ (e) عامّ

Exercise 8 (a) الاجتماع **al-ijtimā9** (b) يومي **yóumī**
(c) شهري **sháhrī** (d) وصول **wuṣūl** (e) جنوب **janūb**
(f) الأسبوع **al-'usbū9** (g) انتخابي **intikhābī** (h) المدرسة **al-mádrasa**
(j) إيطالي **īṭālī** (k) إداري **idārī**

* This picturesque desert-road warning should be taken seriously, especially if visibility is poor. In a collision, most animals fall under the car. But the camel is hit below his knees, with possibly appalling consequences for both man and beast. The stricken and struggling animal, his already considerable weight increased by the impact, comes crashing through the car roof.

The camel deserves respect. He is silent and can be swift. And the desert is his.

Tests

1 Read aloud and translate these words:

(a) الشّيء (b) مسؤولة (c) السّعر
(d) مدخل (e) الانتخاب

2 Arrange these in the order of their size, biggest first:

(a) اليوم (b) السّنة (c) الأسبوع
(d) الشّهر

3 Make a relative, in the indefinite masculine form, from each noun. Give its meaning:

(a) الصّناعة (b) ابتداء (c) الأسبوع
(d) ايطاليا (e) بريطانيا

4 Write:

(a) **at-ta'sīs** (b) **an-nihā'ī** (c) **mas'ūla**
(d) **al-ma<u>kh</u>raj** (e) **ad-du<u>kh</u>ūl**

Review

In this unit we covered seven more joined letters, two of them sun letters with dark sounds; and many useful new words. You also learned how to stress correctly any word in the language.

The next unit gives us the remaining three letters and three 'curiosities', rounding off the alphabetical part of this book.

6

In this unit you will learn

- the remaining three letters, and three special spellings, with their pronunciation,
- the full alphabet in its proper order,
- how Arabic transcribes foreign words.

Letters

1

فـ ف	**fā**
قـ ق	**qāf**

The joined letter فـ ف **fā** represents *f* as in English *fee*. The joined letter قـ ق **qāf**, which we can transcribe as **q**, is pronounced like *k* in English, but as far back in the throat as possible. Say *coo* several times, taking the contact back as far as you can. The result is **q**. The letter ق does *not* represent an English *q* in sound.

The short and full forms are used in the manner known to you. The full form of **fā** is shallow like the ب group, while the full form of **qāf** is deep with a swoop, like ن . Both **fā** and **qāf** are dotted above the ring, in both short and full forms. Write several:

فـ .... ف .... قـ .... ق .... فـ .... ف .... قـ .... ق ....

فِـ .... فَ .... قَـ .... قَ .... فِـ .... فَ .... قَـ .... قَ ....

In Tunisia, Algeria and Morocco you may find ڢـ ڢ for **fā** and ڧـ ڧ for **qāf**; in Morocco you can see signs indicating the city of ڢاس **fās** *Fez*. In this book we use the much commoner forms of the letters, shown in the box.

Since ق has a dark sound, any neighbouring **a** or **ā** is darkened. The dark vowels are dotted in the examples given below. Read and write:

تفتيش **taftīsh** *inspection* .... فنّي **fannī** *technical* ....

سفارة **sifāṛa** *embassy* .... سفير **safīr** *ambassador* ....

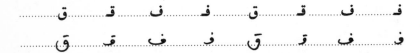

....	رقم	**raqm** *number*	....	مفتوح	**maftūḥ** *open*
....	شرق	**sharq** *east*	....	قف	**qif** *STOP* (on road signs)
....	سوق	**sūq** *market*	....	تقرير	**taqrīr** *report, decision*
....	العراق	**al-9irāq** *Iraq*	....	القاهرة	**al-qāhira** *Cairo*

2

ك ک kāf

The letter ك ک **kāf** represents the sound *k* as in English *book.* It is a tall joined letter, with short and full forms used in the manner known to you. The forms you see here are printed forms; in handwriting the short form is upright, while in the full form the small embellishment ء becomes a hook inside the curve (like the dot of ن , see Unit 1). The differences are shown below:

handwriting: .... *print and type:* ك ک

Write several handwritten forms:

........ك........ک........ك........ک........ك........ک........ك ....ک

....

The 'headstroke' of the short form, and the hook of the long form, serve to make sure that this letter does not get confused with ل ﻟ . You will also meet the printed isolated form ﻙ , not used in handwriting. Read and write:

....	شركة	**sharika** *company*	....	كبير	**kabīr** *big*
....	ممكن	**mumkin** *possible*	....	مكتب	**maktab** *office*
			....	بنك	**bank** *bank*

There are special handwritten forms for the combinations **kāf-alif, kāf-lām** and **kāf-lām-alif**. Copy the handwritten forms from this table:

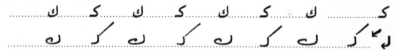

handwriting	*print*
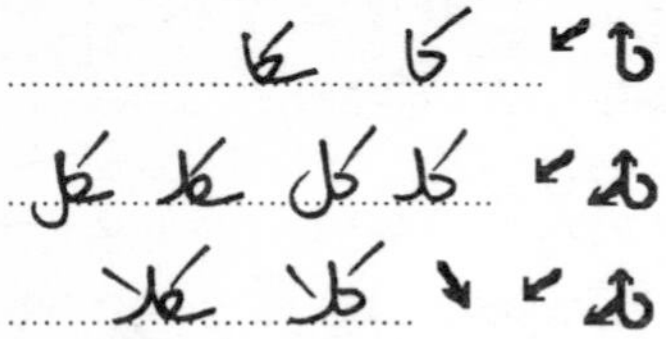	كا ـكا
	كلـ كل ـكلـ\ـكل
	كلا ـكلا

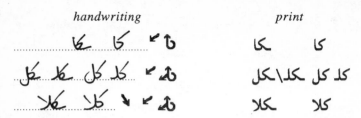

Now ***read and write:***

إمكانية **imkānīya** *possibility* كاتب **kātib** *writer*

مشكلة **mu<u>sh</u>kila** *problem* كلّ **kull** *every, all*

تكليف **taklīf** *cost* كلام **kalām** *speech, speaking*

Exercise 1 Write these new words:

(a) **ak<u>th</u>ar** *more* (b) **<u>sh</u>akl** *form* (c) **kammīya** *quantity*
(d) **miftāḥ** *key* (e) **iqtirāḥ** *proposal*

Exercise 2 Given the word مكتوب **maktūb** *written* as a model, you can easily read words with the same pattern such as مربوط **marbūṭ** *connected*, معلوم **ma9lūm** *known*, منشور **man<u>sh</u>ūr** *published*. Now read these new words, following the model given:

(a) كاتب **kātib** *writer*. Read عامل *worker*, سائق *driver*, ساكن *resident*

(b) كبير **kabīr** *big*. Read كثير *much*, صغير *small*, فقير *poor*, قريب *near*, قليل *little, few*

(c) استقبال **istiqbāl** *reception*. Read استكشاف *exploration*, استثمار *investment*, استعمال *use*, استنكار *rejection*, استقلال *independence*

(d) تفتيش **taftī<u>sh</u>** *inspection* . Read تقسيم *partition*, تحسين *repair*, تعليم *tuition*

(e) مكتب **maktab** *office*. Read مطبخ *kitchen*, متحف *museum*, مشغل *workshop*, مصنع, *factory*, ملعب *playground, playing-field*

(f) ممثّل **muma<u>thth</u>il** *representative*. Read مفتّش *inspector*, مقرّر reporter, مدرّس *instructor*, محرّك *engine*

The answers to these exercises follow paragraph 6 below.

3

ةً اً tanwīn

Now that you have learned the alphabet, here are three curiosities for you. The first two, shown in the box above, are called **tanwīn***, which we can translate as '*en-ing*' or 'providing with *n*'. Here they are in action:

فوراً **fouran** *immediately*   عادةً **9ādatan** *usually*

The one with **alif**, اً, is always pronounced **-an** (short **a**, despite the **alif**), while the one with **tā marbūṭa**, ةً, is pronounced **-atan**. The dots of ة are always written in handwriting for this form. When **tanwīn** is added to the ending **-ī** the combination becomes ...يّاً\...يّةً **-īyan/-īyatan**. We write **tanwīn** only at the end of a word, and it is useful because it marks countless *adverbs*, i.e. words describing verbs or adjectives. In some print, and, alas, in much handwriting, the ً... mark is omitted, leaving us with ا... and ة... which is not very helpful. In this book the ً... is always shown, and you are advised always to write it. The *n* sound is *not* written with ن in this special form.

* There are in fact three **tanwīns**, one for each of the vowels **a**, **i** and **u**; but you will hardly ever see the last two, and they need not concern us. The full name of the useful one shown here is **alif tanwīn**. We can call it simply **tanwīn**.

Read and write:

.... رسمياً **rasmīyan** *officially* .... كثيراً **kathīran** *greatly*

.... قليلاً **qalīlan** *a little* .... مثلاً **mathalan** *for example*

.... خاصّةً **khāssatan** *specially*

4

ى alif maqṣūra

This one is our third curiosity. In some words you will see a final **yā**, without the dots, which is not pronounced **-ī** at all, but which sounds **-a**, just like final ا **alif**. This form is called **alif maqṣūra**. It occurs in only a few words. Pronounce it **-a**. This ‘curiosity’ can be confusing.

The situation is not helped by the fact that ي proper (the one that is pronounced **-ī**), when standing alone, is often printed and handwritten without its dots: you will, for example, see مصرى for مصري **miṣrī**.

Two things are worth noting, and they offer some help:

- when you see ى it is much more likely to be **yā** (sounded **-ī**) which is much more common than **alif maqṣūra** (sounded **-a**),
- **alif maqṣūra** occurs only at the end of a word, nowhere else.

Throughout this book we write ي for isolated **yā** and ى only for **alif maqsūra**. You are recommended to do the same, to make your handwriting clear.

Read and write:

..........الى..إلى **ila** *to* ....على..على **9ala** *on*

..........مستشفى..مستشفى **musta<u>sh</u>fa** *hospital*

Exercise 3 Which way, right or left, to (a) *school*, (b) *hospital*, (c) *airport*, (d) *market*? Read the words aloud:

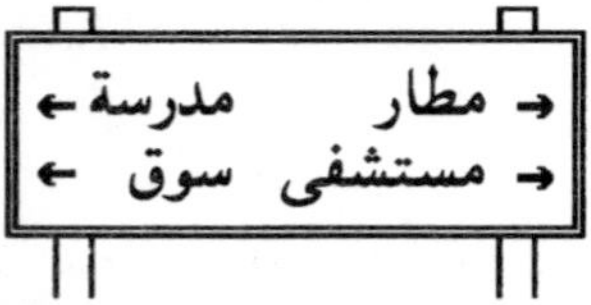

The answers to this exercise follow paragraph 6 below.

Alphabet

5 Here is the whole alphabet, in its Arabic order. Read from the middle outwards, as you always should when you have parallel Arabic and English columns: ← →

ا	**alif**
ب ت ث	**bā tā <u>th</u>ā**
ج ح خ	**jīm ḥā <u>kh</u>ā**

د ذ	**dāl dhāl**
ر ز	**rā zayy**
س ش	**sīn shīn**
ص ض	**ṣād ḍād**
ط ظ	**ṭā ẓā**
ع غ	**9ayn ghayn**
ف ق ك	**fā qāf kāf**
ل م ن	**lām mīm nūn**
ه و ي	**hā wow yā**

Special letters, and signs not found in the alphabet, are usually listed as follows:

آ, أ and إ	with ا
ة	with ه
ؤ	with ا or و
ئـ\ئ	with ا or ي
ى	with ي
...ً	is disregarded

Using this order, you can look up a proper name or a department etc. in a list or directory such as a telephone book or street index; also in the vocabulary in this book. You can also use a dictionary, provided you use one of the newer ones which list alphabetically by *words*: examples are Steingass' Arabic-English Dictionary published by Khayat in Beirut, or a later edition of 'Al-Mawrid', Arabic-English, published by Dar al-Ilm li-l-Malayin, also of Beirut.

If you understand German, you can use Langenscheidt's Arabic-German/German-Arabic dictionary, either the pocket or the desk edition. This is also arranged alphabetically by words, with transcription.

Avoid older Arabic-English dictionaries: they may be good, but they list by *roots*, and you have to know Arabic grammar well to find your word.

The vocabularies in this book are arranged alphabetically by words.

Exercise 4 Put these customer files in their right alphabetical order:

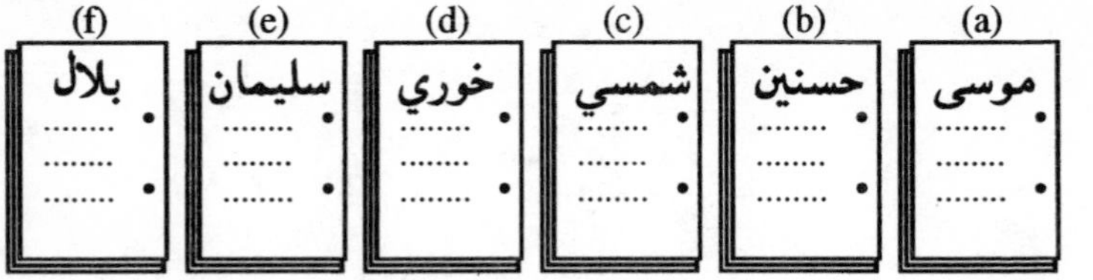

Match the transcriptions to the names: **mūsa**, **bilāl**, **ḥasanayn**, **shamsī**, **sulaymān**, **khūrī**.

Now imagine opening three fresh files in the names of (g) **zaydān**, (h) **abūbakr** and (j) **nūrī**. Write these names and put them in alphabetical order with the others.

The answers to this exercise follow paragraph 6 below.

Arabic Transcription

6 There is no standard Arabic transcription for foreign words. But the following principles seem generally to be followed.

Little distinction is made between foreign long and short vowels: ا is used for long and short *a*, و for long and short *u* and *o*, and ي for long and short *e* and *i*.

v is usually transcribed either with ف or the artificial letter ڤ ; *p* either with ب or the Persian/Urdu letter پ ; *g* with ك or ج, and *ch* with the Persian/Urdu letter چ :

فيينا\ڤيينا **viyēnā** *Vienna* باريس **pārīs** *Paris*

جنيف **jinēv** (Fr. *Genève*) *Geneva* روما **rōma** *Rome*

تلفون\تليفون **tilifōn/tilīfōn** *telephone* كمبيوتر **kampyūtir** *computer*

أوتوبيس **otobīs** (Fr. *autobus*) *bus* أوتيل **ōtēl** (Fr. *hôtel*) *hotel*

As you know, in Egypt ج is pronounced like hard English *g* (see Unit 5), so you often see چ for **j** in foreign names in Egypt: چاكارتا Jakarta.

Initial *s* followed by a consonant other than *w* is transcribed as اسـ.. :

اسكتلندا **iskotlanda** Scotland, but: سويسرا **swisira** Switzerland.

When reading a commercial sign, remember that it is possibly not Arabic at all. Try reading it aloud, especially if it has no recognisable Arabic shape. I used to enjoy watching people puzzle over a shop sign in the Arabian Gulf which read **فيش اند چيپس**; it sometimes took them a minute to realise that they could go inside and order the local equivalent of cod-and-fries, and even wash it down with a cool **فانتا**, a **سيڤن آپ** or a **بيبسي كولا**.

Oil products

Answers to Exercises

Exercise 1 (a) **اكثر** (b) **شكل** (c) **كمّية** (d) **مفتاح** (e) **اقتراح**

Exercise 2 (a) **9āmil, sā'iq, sākin**
(b) **kathīr, ṣaghīr, faqīr, qarīb, qalīl**
(c) **istikshāf, istithmār, isti9māl, istinkār, istiqlāl**
(d) **taqsīm, taḥsīn, ta9līm**
(e) **maṭbakh, mathaf, mashghal, maṣna9, mal9ab**
(f) **mufattish, muqarrir, mudarris, muḥarrik**

Exercise 3 (a) **مدرسة madrasa**, left; (b) **مستشفى mustashfa**, right; (c) **مطار maṭār**, right; (d) **سوق sūq**, left.

Exercise 4 (f) **bilāl** (b) **ḥasanayn** (d) **khūrī** (e) **sulaymān** (c) **shamsī** (a) **mūsa**.
(g) **زيدان** goes before (e), (h) **ابوبكر** goes first, and (j) **نوري** goes last.

Tests

1 Read aloud and translate:

(a) صناعة (b) مطار (c) مسؤول
(d) وزارة (e) إدارة (f) أخبار
(g) احتجاج (h) شركة (j) أو
(k) سوق (m) مثلاً (n) مستشفى

2 Rewrite the word, filling in the missing letter. Read your answer aloud.

(a) مـ..ـلّم (b) مـ..تب (c) فور...
(d) تـ..سيس (e) ابتـ..ائي

3 You certainly know these international brand names. Read them aloud:

(a) كوداك (b) آي بي إم (c) مـوبيل
(d) ميشلين (e) بيجو*

*(e) difficult. Every single letter in this French name is at best an approximation.

> **Review**
>
> We have now completed the alphabet and the various signs commonly used in writing.
>
> If you are in an Arab country while working through this book, you should already be able to make sense of some of the words shown on signs and notices around you.

7

In this unit you will learn

- how to make words *dual* (two of a kind) and *plural* (more than two of a kind),
- how to read and write figures.

Word Forms

1 Dual

You will occasionally see the ending ...ين **-ayn** or ...ان **-ān** added to a word. This is the so-called 'dual' ending, and it means 'two'. English uses a number for 'two'; Arabic uses an ending.

A final ة on the original word changes to ت , and a final ى (**alif maqṣura**, see Unit 6 paragraph 4) changes to ي , before the dual ending is added.

The relative ending ي together with the dual ending becomes ...يين **-īyayn** or ...يان **-īyān**. ***Read and write:***

مديران مديران **mudirān** مديرين مديرين **mudirayn**

مكتبان مكتبان **maktabān** مكتبين مكتبين **maktabayn**

وزارتان وزارتان **wizāratān** وزارتين وزارتين **wizāratayn**

شركتان شركتان **sharikatān** شركتين شركتين **sharikatayn**

لبنانيان لبنانيين لبنانيين\لبنانيان **lubnānīyayn/lubnānīyān**

مستشفيين مستشفيين **mustashfayayn**

مستشفيان مستشفيان **mustashfayān**

two directors, two offices, two ministries, two companies, two Lebanese (m.), *two hospitals*

The two endings are not interchangeable. You will find the ...ين **-ayn** series (the first one shown) much more common, and you should use it for preference when in doubt. We will have some guidelines later.

The dual ending is always *stressed*: **-áyn/-ấn**.

2 Plural endings

Remember that whereas for English 'plural' means 'more than one', for Arabic it means 'more than *two*'.

There are two endings we can add to words to make them plural (pl.).

The commonest plural ending you will meet is ...ات . This is known as the *feminine* plural ending.

This is added to almost all nouns ending in ة , whatever their meaning (the ة is dropped before the plural ending is added), and to many nouns denoting things, places or ideas, whatever their ending.

It is also added to the very few nouns ending in ى , which of course changes to ي before the plural ending is added. ***Read and write:***

انتخابات انتخابات **intikhābāt** — انتخاب انتخاب **intikhāb**

شركات شركات **sharikāt** — شركة شركة **sharika**

معلّمات معلّمات **mu9allimāt** — معلّمة معلّمة **mu9allima**

مستشفى مستشفى **mustashfa**

مستشفيات مستشفيات **mustashfayāt**

election(s), company/-ies, teacher(s) (f.), *hospital(s)*

The second commonest plural ending is ...ين **-īn**, with its rarer variant ...ون **-ūn**.

This ending is added only to a few words denoting male persons. It is known as the *masculine* plural ending.

The relative ending ي together with this plural ending becomes ...يين **-īyīn** (less commonly, ...يون **-īyūn**). ***Read and write:***

معلّمون معلّمون **mu9allimūn** — معلّمين معلّمين **mu9allimīn**

ممثّلون ممثّلون **mumaththilūn** — ممثّلين ممثّلين **mumaththilīn**

مفتّشون مفتّشون **mufattishūn** — مفتّشين مفتّشين **mufattishīn**

إيطاليون ايطاليون **īṭālīyūn** — إيطاليين ايطاليين **īṭālīyīn**

teacher(s), representative(s), inspector(s), Italian(s) - all masculine.

As with the dual, so the two masculine plural endings are not interchangeable. The **ين... -īn** series is much more common, and you should use it for preference when in doubt. We will have some guidelines later.

The masculine plural ending is always *stressed*: **-ī́n/-ū́n**.

3 Irregular plurals

Very many words make their plurals not by adding an ending, but by changing their internal shape. We have this phenomenon with a few English words; consider the singular 'man' with its plural 'men', or 'mouse' and 'mice'. Irregular plural patterns are very common in Arabic. Many such patterns exist, and, unfortunately for us, we can give no rules. An irregular plural form has to be learned together with its singular.

A few important patterns are listed below, with a model word for each pattern.

It looks a formidable list. *Don't* try to learn it: simply take note that such patterns exist, and use the list for reference. The important thing is that when you meet an unfamiliar irregular plural, you check whether you know a singular noun with the same consonants in the same order. If you do, there is a good chance that you have broken the code and identified the meaning. Using a foreign language often involves astute detective work and intelligent guessing.

Read and write the examples:

(a) model **a<u>kh</u>bār**:

irregular plural			*singular*		
اخبار	أخبار	**a<u>kh</u>bār**	خبر	خبر	**<u>kh</u>abar** *news items*
انباء	أنباء	**anbā'**	نبأ	نبأ	**naba'** *news items*
اسعار	أسعار	**as9ār**	سعر	سعر	**si9r** *price*
اخطار	أخطار	**a<u>kh</u>ṭār**	خطر	خطر	**<u>kh</u>aṭar** *danger*
اشياء	أشياء	**a<u>sh</u>yā'**	شيء	شيء	**<u>sh</u>ay'** *thing*
افلام	أفلام	**aflām**	فلم	فلم	**film** *film*

(b) model **buyūt**:

بيوت	بيوت	**buyūt**	بيت	بيت	**bayt** *house*
خطوط	خطوط	**<u>kh</u>uṭūṭ**	خطّ	خطّ	**<u>kh</u>aṭṭ** *line*
بنوك	بنوك	**bunūk**	بنك	بنك	**bank** *bank*
هنود	هنود	**hunūd**	هندي	هندي	**hindī** *Indian*

(c) model **madāris**:

مدارس	مدارس	**madāris**	مدرسة	مدرسة	**madrasa** *school*
مشاكل	مشاكل	**ma<u>sh</u>ākil**	مشكلة	مشكلة	**mu<u>sh</u>kila** *problem*
مكاتب	مكاتب	**makātib**	مكتب	مكتب	**maktab** *office*
مخارج	مخارج	**ma<u>kh</u>ārij**	مخرج	مخرج	**ma<u>kh</u>raj** *exit*
مداخل	مداخل	**madā<u>kh</u>il**	مدخل	مدخل	**mad<u>kh</u>al** *entrance*

(d) model **asābī9**:

اسابيع	أسابيع	**asābī9**	اسبوع	أسبوع	**usbū9** *week*
مفاتيح	مفاتيح	**mafātiḥ**	مفتاح	مفتاح	**miftāḥ** *key*

(e) model **mudarā'**:

مدراء	مدراء	**mudarā'**	مدير	مدير	**mudīr** *director*
وزراء	وزراء	**wuzarā'**	وزير	وزير	**wazīr** *minister*

(f) model **9arab**:

عرب	عرب	**9arab**	عربي	عربي	**9arabī** *Arab, Arabic, Arabian*
انجليز	إنجليز	**ingilīz**	انجليزى	إنجليزي	**ingilīzī** *English, British*
يهود	يهود	**yahūd**	يهودي	يهودي	**yahūdī** *Jew(ish)*

and many other patterns.

Some words have alternative plurals, one with an ending, one irregular; or even two irregular forms. Sometimes the alternatives have different meanings. An example is تقرير **taqrīr** *report, decision*, plurals تقارير **taqārīr** *reports*, تقريرات **taqrīrāt** *decisions.*

Another important word with alternative plural forms is أميركي **amayrkī** *American*, plurals أميركيين\...يون **amayrkīyīn/-īyūn** or أميركان **amayrkān**.

Three final things to note about plural and dual forms:

- All the duals and plurals can be made definite with the article, as usual: المدراء, المعلّمين, الشّركات, المديرين.
- When a noun has a regular plural, we add the masculine ending (...ين\...ون) to a noun denoting a male person, or to show mixed company, male and female; we add the feminine regular ending (...ات) to a noun denoting a female person, *and* to a noun denoting anything other than a person.
- The **-ayn** ending and the **-īn** ending are both written ...ين . There can be confusion. There is a means of marking the difference, but you never see it in use. In general, read **-īn** if in doubt.

In the rest of this book, irregular plurals of new words will be given with the singular, so: بيت بيوت **bayt buyūt**. Where no plural is marked, it is regular, i.e. is formed with an ending, as shown above.

Exercise 1 Here are some plurals. Give the singular form of the word:

(a) مدراء (b) سيّارات (c) تلفونات (d) مفتّشين (e) خطوط

Exercise 2 Put the words together in singular/plural pairs:

بنايات، مدير، مفتّش، بناية، وزراء، وزارات، شركات، بيوت مدراء، مفتّشين، وزير، معلّمة، وزارة، شركة، معلّمات، بيت.

Exercise 3 Make the relative form, in the feminine:

(a) أميركا* (b) وطن (c) باكستان* (d) إسرائيل* (e) العراق

* New foreign words. Easy, if you say them aloud.

Exercise 4 (a), (b) and (c) below are signs and notices which we have read before. Can you fill in the missing captions? Having done that, read, pronounce and translate the new sign, (d):

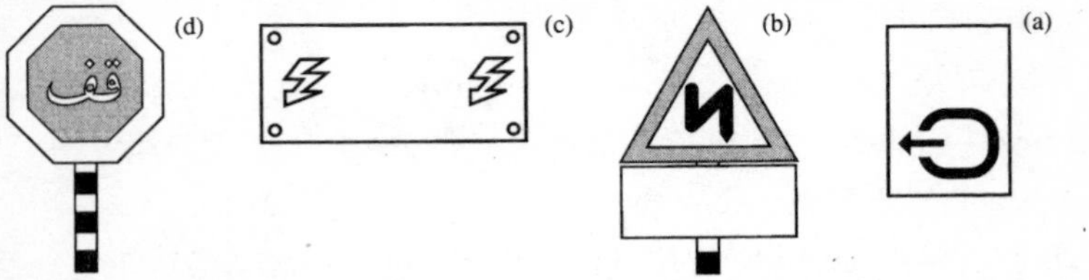

Exercise 5 Look back at Unit 6, Exercise 2. Read these new words, following the model given:

(a) كتّاب **kuttāb** *writers*. Read زوّار *visitors*, عمّال *workmen*, نوّاب *deputies*.

(b) مكتوب **maktūb** *written*. Read ممنوع *prohibited*, مطبوع *printed*, معروف *known*, مكتوم *confidential*.

(c) مدرسة **madrasa** *school*. Read مكتب *library/bookshop*, محكمة *law-court*.

(d) سياحة **siyāha** *tourism*. Read نجارة *carpentry*, سباكة *plumbing*, خياطة *sewing*.

The answers to these exercises follow paragraph 4 below.

Figures

4 Figures are written as follows. Most important: they are written from *left to right*, like European figures. Write the handwritten forms shown below the printed forms:

→→

1	١	١	١	2	٢	٢	٢
	١	١	١		٢	٢	٢
3	٣	٣	٣	4	٤	٤	٤
	٣	٣	٣		٤	٤	٤
5	٥	٥	٥	6	٦	٦	٦
	٥	٥	٥		٦	٦	٦

7	٧	٧	٧	8	٨	٨	٨
	٧	٧	٧		٨	٨	٨
9	٩	٩	٩	0	٠	٠	٠
	٩	٩	٩		٠	٠	٠

Be careful with handwritten figures ٢ (٢) and ٢ or ٣ (٣). Many people write ٣ for extra clarity. It is not wrong to copy the printed forms in handwriting if you prefer; though some Arabs may read your ٢ as a handwritten ٣.

Don't confuse ٥ (5) with ٠ (0).

When figures occur with letters or symbols, they should be read like this: ٥٩٨ ب as *598 B*; ٪٦٤ as *64%*. Reading in both directions needs a little practice.

In Morocco, Algeria, Tunisia and Libya the European figures are used.

There is more about numbers, including how they are pronounced, in Unit 13.

Exercise 6 Write in Arabic figures:

(a) *2487* (b) *503* (c) *1999* (d) *1420* (e) *2006*

Exercise 7 Write in European figures:

٤٠٥ (e) ١٠٠٠ (d) ٢٠٥٧ (c) ١٦٢ (b) ٤٣٨٥ (a)

Exercise 8 Copy in Arabic figures and letters these car number-plates in handwriting. Then put them into European figures and letters:

(c)

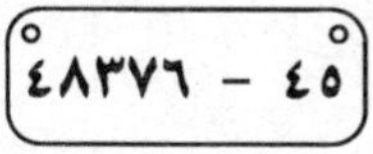

(b)

(a)

The answers to these exercises are on the next page.

Answers to Exercises

Exercise 1 (a) مدير (b) سيّارة (c) تلفون (d) مفتّش (e) خطّ

Exercise 2

بناية، بنايات؛ مدير، مدراء؛ مفتّش، مفتّشين؛ وزير، وزراء؛
وزارة، وزارات؛ شركة، شركات؛ بيت، بيوت؛ معلّمة، معلّمات.

Exercise 3 (a) أميركية (b) وطنية (c) باكستانية (d) إسرائيلية
(e) عراقية

Exercise 4 (a) مخرج (b) تمهّل (c) خطر (d) **qif** *STOP*

Exercise 5 (a) **zuwwār, 9ummāl, nuwwāb**
(b) **mamnū9, maṭbū9, ma9rūf, maktūm**
(c) **maktaba, maḥkama**
(d) **nijāra, sibāka, <u>kh</u>iyāṭa**

Exercise 6 (a) ٢٤٨٧ (b) ٥٠٣ (c) ١٩٩٩ (d) ١٤٢٠
(e) ٢٠٠٦

Exercise 7 (a) *4385* (b) *162* (c) *2057* (d) *1000* (e) *405*

Exercise 8 (a) س ٤٨٩٢٣ *48923 S* (b) ٤٨٣٧٦-٤٥ *48376-45*
(c) ٧٩-٦٣٢٧ *79 6327*

Tests

1 Read aloud and translate:

(a) العراق	(b) القاهرة	(c) شركة
(d) ممكن	(e) زيارة	(f) إداري
(g) ممثّلين	(h) السّوريين	(j) محكمة
(k) أجنبي	(m) مدارس	(n) الانتخابات

2 Arrange these iregular plurals into groups, each group with its model (which is included to help you). Don't worry about the words you don't know; it is the pattern which counts:

مشاكل، أسابيع، خطوط، ظروف، مطاعم، أرقام، عواصم،
أموال، وزراء، بيوت، مبالغ، مدراء، أخبار، محاكم، أساليب،
وكلاء، أفكار، مدارس، بنوك.

3 Make the masculine plural relative, in the indefinite form (e.g. لبنانيين), from each word:

(a) سوريا (b) إيران (c) مصر
(d) العراق (e) الكويت*

*(e) unfair - we haven't done this proper name. But it is familiar and you can handle it. Just follow the rules.

4 Make these words plural. They all follow the feminine regular pattern:

(a) البناية (b) السفارة (c) مستشفى
(d) كمبيوتر (e) أوتيل (f) معلّمة
(g) المطار (h) منظّمة (j) شركة
(k) إمكانية (m) الزيارة (n) انتخاب

Review

We have learned the dual and the plural, regular and irregular. Don't be discouraged by the variety of irregular plurals; Arabs often have similar difficulty. The commonest patterns become more familiar with practice.

Next we learn some of the word-patterns which characterise Arabic - and which help us to find our way around a language whose words are very different from our own.

8

In this unit you will learn

- three important forms derived from verbs,
- something about other writing styles.

Verbal Forms

1 Participles

Think of English words like 'writer', 'writing', 'written'. The first one names a person *doing an action*; the second describes such a person. The third describes a thing *suffering an action.*

All three are derived from a verb (in this case *to write*), but they are not verbs themselves. They are either *nouns* or *adjectives* (look back to Unit 4, paragraph 4 if you are unsure of these terms).

Arabic has such words too, and they are numerous and useful. We call them **participles**. The ones referring to a *person or thing doing an action* (*writer, writing* in English) are called **active participles**. The ones referring to a *person or thing suffering an action* (*written* in English) are called **passive participles**.

Both active and passive varieties can be used either as nouns or as adjectives, as long as the words make sense.

Arabic participles have recognisable patterns, fortunately not too many to learn. Here are the main ones, grouped according to a model, with examples, which you will find useful. Obviously, a verb has both active and passive participles only where both would make sense or be useful. For most verbs, only one of the two is in common use. The columns shown below (active on the left, passive on the right) reflect this fact.

Approach this list in the same way as you did the irregular plural patterns listed in Unit 7. What is familiar will stick in your memory straight away, giving you the pattern. Practice, and inquisitiveness, will help you to apply the pattern more widely.

Read and write (there is, alas, no room to show the handwriting here):

Active Participle ('doing')	Passive Participle ('suffering')
(a) model **kātib** (active), **maktūb** (passive):	
كاتب كتّاب **kātib kuttāb** *writer, clerk*	مكتوب **maktūb** *written*
سائق **sā'iq** *driver*	
عامل عمّال **9āmil 9ummāl** *workman*	
لازم **lāzim** *necessary*	
حاضر **ḥāḍir** *present, ready*	
	مفتوح **maftūḥ** *open(ed)*
	ممنوع **mamnū9** *prohibited*
	مشغول **mashghūl** *busy ('busied')*
	معلومات **ma9lumāt** *('things known') information*
	محفوظ **maḥfūẓ** *reserved*
(b) model **mumaththil** (active), **mumaththal** (passive):	
ممثّل **mumaththil** *representative*	ممثّل **mumaththal** *represented*
مفتّش **mufattish** *inspector*	
معلّم **mu9allim** *teacher*	
مدرّس **mudarris** *instructor*	
مقرّر **muqarrir** *reporter*	مقرّر **muqarrar** *decided*
(c) model **musā9id** (active; no common passives):	
مساعد **musā9id** *assistant*	
مسافر **musāfir** *traveller*	
محامي **muḥāmī** *lawyer*	
محاسب **muḥāsib** *accountant*	
مناسب **munāsib** *appropriate*	
(d) model **mursil** (active), **mursal** (passive):	
مرسل **mursil** *sender*	مرسل **mursal** *sent*
معطي **mu9ṭī** *donor*	
مفيد **mufīd** *useful*	
مهمّ **muhimm** *important*	

(e) model **muntakh*i*b** (active), **muntakh*a*b** (passive):

منتخب **muntakhib** *elector*	منتخب **muntakhab** *elected*
مشترك **mushtarik** *participant*	مشترك **mushtarak** *joint, common*
متّحد **muttaḥid** *united*	
منتظر **muntaẓir** *waiting for*	منتظر **muntaẓar** *awaited*

(f) model **mustakhd*i*m** (active), **mustakhd*a*m** (passive):

مستخدم **mustakhdim** *employer*	مستخدم **mustakhdam** *employed*
مستقبل **mustaqbil** *(radio, TV) receiver*	مستقبل **mustaqbal** *future*
مستعدّ ل **musta9idd li-** *ready for*	

You can see that

- a few active participles of model (a) have an irregular plural, in the masculine form, almost all other participles (passive of model (a), and active and passive of models (b) to (f)) having regular plurals.
- in models (b) to (f), the only difference in form between the active and passive forms is in the last vowel: **-i-** for the active, **-a-** for the passive. Unfortunately, everyday Arabic writing does not show this important difference. There is a way of marking it, but this is seldom used outside school textbooks. We have to be guided by the context.

The participle can be made feminine and/or plural, as usual:

معلّمة **mu9allima** *teacher* (f.)   سائقين **sā'iqīn** *drivers*

Exercise 1 Read aloud the participles listed after each model:
(a) model كاتب: وارد *arriving*, طالب *student*, كامل *complete*, عارف *knowing*
(c) model مساعد: محافظ *conservative*, مقابل *facing*
(f) model مستخدم: مستعمل *user*, مستأجر *tenant*, مستثمر *investor*
What is the last vowel in all these participles? How do you know?

Exercise 2 Read aloud these passive participles:
مكسور *broken*, مستنكر *rejected*, مسلّح *armed*, مقترح *proposed*

The answers to these exercises follow paragraph 4 below.

Verbal Nouns

2 Think of the English word 'inspection'. It comes from a verb ('to inspect') but is itself a noun. It denotes the *activity* of the verb. Arabic has countless nouns of this kind; we call them **verbal nouns**. We know the verbal noun *inspection* in Arabic, from Unit 6: it is **تفتيش** **taftīsh**.

Verbal nouns are important in Arabic. We meet them constantly in notices etc. The ones corresponding to the group (a) participles (model كاتب\مكتوب) are irregular in form, but groups (b) to (f), corresponding to the participle groups (b) to (f), are regular, following known models in the same way as do the participles.

The following list is *not* intended for learning outright. Treat it mainly as reference material; some of it is familiar already. ***Read and write:***

(a) irregular (several patterns are found; the words are best learned simply as nouns):

كتابه	كتابة	**kitāba** (the act of) *writing*
وصول	وصول	**wuṣūl** *arrival*
عمل اعمال	عمل أعمال	**9amal a9māl** *work*

(b) model **taftīsh**:

تفتيش	تفتيش	**taftīsh** *inspection*
تعليم	تعليم	**ta9līm** *tuition, education*
تنظيم	تنظيم	**tanẓīm** (act of) *organisation*
تقرير	تقرير	**taqrīr** *report, decision*

(c) model **musā9ada**:

مساعده	مساعدة	**musā9ada** *help*
محاسبات	محاسبات	**muḥāsabāt** (pl.) *accounts*
مغادره	مغادرة	**mughādara** *departure*

(d) model **irsāl**:

ارسال إرسال **irsāl** *despatch*

اداره إدارة **idāra** *administration*

اضراب إضراب **iḍrāb** *strike*

(e) model **intikhāb**:

انتخاب انتخاب **intikhāb** *election*

اشتراك اشتراك **ishtirāk** *participation*

انتظار انتظار **intiẓār** *wait(ing)*

(f) model **istikhdām**:

استخدام استخدام **istikhdām** *employment, recruitment*

استقبال استقبال **istiqbāl** *reception*

These nouns can of course form *relatives* (Unit 4) by adding **...ـي**.
Read and write:

تعليمي تعليمي **ta9līmī** *educational, tutorial*

الاشتراكيين الاشتراكيين **al-ishtirākīyīn** *the socialists*

Abstract Nouns

3 You will also find *abstract* nouns (i.e. nouns denoting a quality or state) ending in **...ية -īya**. These are in fact feminine relatives, but used only as nouns. ***Read and write***, and remember if you can, such useful abstracts as:

الاشتراكيه الاشتراكية **al-ishtirākīya** *socialism*

الدموقراطيه الدّموقراطية **ad-dimuqrāṭīya** *democracy*

Other Written Styles

4 Just as in our alphabet, so in the Arabic alphabet there are various styles or typefaces in use. Here are all the letter families, first in the style used in this book; then in a newspaper style; then in typewriting; then in two decorative styles used on buildings and monuments:

اءبب جج درسس صص ط ععع ع فف ق كك لل مم نن ههه ه و يي ي

اءبب جج درسس صص ط ععع ع فف ق كك لل مم نن ههه ه ويي ي

اءبب جج درسس صص ط ععع ع فف ق كك لل مم نن ههه ه و يي ى

اءبب جج درسس صص ط ععع ع فف ق كك لل مم نن ههه ه ويي ي

اءبب جج درسس صص ط ععع ع فف ق كك لل مم نن ههه ه ويي ي

Many Arabs use a handwriting style with abbreviated shapes for certain dotted letters standing at the end of a word or alone. Reading this kind of handwriting is much easier if we know these shapes. Here are the important ones:

Exercise 3 Read aloud these verbal nouns:
تجديد *renewal,* استقلال *independence,* تدريس *instruction,* اجتماع *meeting,* إصلاح *reform,* تمويل *financing,* مناسبة *occasion,* انتقال *transfer*

The answers to this exercise are immediately below.

Answers to Exercises

Exercise 1 (a) **wārid, ṭālib, kāmil, 9ārif**
(c) **muḥāfiẓ, muqābil**
(f) **musta9mil, musta'jir, mustathmir**
The last vowel is **i**, since from their meaning the participles are active.

Exercise 2 maksūr, mustankar, musallaḥ, muqtaraḥ

Exercise 3 tajdīd, istiqlāl, tadrīs, ijtimā9, iṣlāḥ, tamwīl, munāsaba, intiqāl

Tests

1 These are words which we have not studied. Pronounce each one and identify it either as a masculine active participle or a verbal noun. Don't worry about the meaning; it is the form that counts:

(a) تقديم (b) راكب (c) مراسل
(d) إنذار (e) مستعلم (f) شامل
(g) افتتاح (h) سامع (j) مدرّس
(k) استثمار

2 Write:

(a) **munāsiba** (b) **inti<u>kh</u>ābī** (c) **muqarrirīn**
(d) **9ummāl** (e) **tanẓīm**

3 Here are five active participles. Give the corresponding verbal nouns. Read aloud and translate the participles and verbal nouns:

(a) مفتّش (b) مشترك (c) مرسل
(d) مساعد (e) مستقبل

4 Read aloud:

(a) (b) مدرسة للبنات
(c) مصر والعراق (d) ايران
(e) القاهرة

> ### Review
>
> Participles and verbal nouns are forms which you will see in abundance on signs and the like. Being able to identify such words will help you to pronounce correctly, and to write down for future use, many new ones which you will meet. Working out their meaning will also be easier.
>
> We have finished our study of separate words. We now move on to expressions ('structures') containing two or more words, very many of these words being like the ones you have just studied.

9

In this unit you will learn

- more about masculine and feminine nouns,
- the first basic structure, linking a noun and an adjective,
- the possessive.

New Words: المواصلات al-muwāṣalāt *Communications*

1

Essential Vocabulary

أجنبي أجانب **ajnabī ajānib** *foreign*	راديو **rādiō** *radio*
إصدار **iṣdār** *issue, issuing*	رسالة **risāla** *letter*
إعلان **i9lān** *anouncement, notice, advertisement*	رسمي **rasmī** *official*
	شخصي **shakhṣī** *personal*
بلاد بلدان **bilād buldān** *country*	صورة صور **ṣūra ṣuwar** *picture, photograph*
تجارة **tijāra** *trade*	
تليفزيون **tilivizyūn** *television*	طويل طوال **ṭawīl ṭiwāl** *long*
جديد جدد **jadīd judud** *new*	علاقات **9alāqāt** *relations*
جميل **jamīl** *beautiful*	قصير قصار **qaṣīr qiṣār** *short*
حكومة **hukūma** *government*	ممتاز **mumtāz** *excellent*

Reference Vocabulary

بريد **barīd** *mail*	لغة **lugha** *language*
تقديم **taqdīm** *presentation*	مجتهد **mujtahid** *hardworking*
جوّي **jawwī** *air* (adjective)	مجلّة **majalla** *magazine*
حديث حداث **hadīth hidāth** *modern*	محلّي **maḥallī** *local*
خطاب أخطبة **khiṭāb akhṭiba** *speech*	مراسل **murāsil** *correspondent*
زميل زملاء **zamīl zumalā'** *colleague* (m.)	معرض معارض **ma9riḍ ma9āriḍ** *exhibition*
صحافة **ṣiḥāfa** *press*	مقالة **maqāla** (press) *article*
صحفي **ṣuḥufī** *journalist*	ملوّن **mulawwan** *coloured*
صحيفة صحف* **ṣaḥīfa ṣuḥuf** *newspaper*	مندوب **mandūb** *delegate*
	مؤتمر **mu'tamar** *conference*
قراءة **qirā'a** (act of) *reading*	نصّ نصوص **naṣṣ nuṣūṣ** *text*

* If you take to speaking your Arabic (and why not?) use the popular spoken word for 'newspaper', جريدة جرائد **jarīda jarā'id**. The word صحيفة is used only in writing.

Basic Structures, 1: The Description

2 Write these two words:

إعلان اعلان **i9lān** *announcement*

هامّ هامّ **hāmm** *important*

إعلان is a *noun*. هامّ is an *adjective*. (Look back to Unit 4, paragraph 4 for these terms, if you need to.) Now write the two words together, *noun first*. We get the expression

إعلان هامّ اعلان هامّ *an important announcement*

This type of expression is our first basic structure, which we can call a **description**. It is very common, and in any Arab town you will see examples all around you in advertisements, notices and the like.

You will remember that Arabic has no word for *a* or *an*. Note also that, in contrast to the English, the Arabic adjective *follows* the noun.

Now ***read and write*** a few more descriptions (remember that relatives - Unit 4 - can be used as adjectives):

كاتب لبناني كاتب لبناني *a Lebanese writer*

خطاب طويل خطاب طويل **khiṭāb ṭawīl** *a long speech*

مقرّر مشغول مقرّر مشغول **(muqarrir)** *a busy reporter*

إعلان عامّ اعلان عامّ *a public notice*

صحفي مصري صحفي مصري **(ṣuḥufī)** *an Egyptian journalist*

Now ***read and write*** *an Egyptian (woman) journalist*. Watch what happens to the adjective:

صحفية مصرية صحفية مصرية *an Egyptian journalist*

The adjective assumes the feminine form too; it is said to *agree* with the feminine noun. ***Read and write*** *an Egyptian newspaper*:

صحيفة مصرية (ṣaḥīfa)

In English, we generally apply the concept of masculine or feminine only to nouns denoting people or higher animals (one possible exception being *she* for a ship or a boat); we regard other nouns as *it* or *neuter*. Arabic has no neuter; *all* nouns, including those for things, places and ideas, are either masculine or feminine (صحيفة, shown above, is feminine). For our purposes, the rules for Arabic nouns are simple:

- nouns for male people and male animals are masculine; nouns for female people and female animals are feminine,
- nouns ending in ة denoting things, places and ideas are feminine; nouns (with any ending) denoting towns, and most countries, are also feminine. Other nouns for things, places and ideas are masculine.

(There is a handful of exceptions, none important enough to concern us.)

With this in mind, ***read and write*** this series of feminine descriptions:

صحفية مشغولة *a busy newswoman*

رسالة رسمية **risāla rasmīya** *an official letter*

صورة جميلة **ṣūra jamīla** *a beautiful picture*

صحيفة عربية *an Arabic newspaper*

All the examples given so far have been indefinite. How do we make a definite description? Given that we make the adjective agree with the noun in gender (m. or f.), it is logical that we make it agree *in definition too*, i.e. indefinite adjective for an indefinite noun, definite adjective for a definite noun. We do just that. ***Read and write:***

الكاتب اللبناني *the Lebanese writer* (m.)

المقرّر المشغول *the busy reporter* (m.)

النصّ الطويل **(an-naṣṣ)** *the long text* (m.)

الصحافة الغربية **aṣ-ṣiḥāfa l-gharbīya***
the western press (f.)

الرساله الطويله الرسالة الطويلة **ar-risāla ṭ-ṭawīla***
the long letter (f.)

المجلّه الجديده المجلّة الجديدة **al-majalla l-jadīda***
the new magazine (f.)

We apply to adjectives the same rules for adding the article **الـ...** (assimilation to sun letters etc., Units 2 and 3) as for nouns.

* Remember that the 'weak' **a-** of the article is dropped after a vowel. It is easiest to pronounce the vowelless article as part of the preceding word: **as-siḥāfa‿l-gharbīya** (etc.).

A proper name (*Egypt, Ahmad*) is always definite, even if it has no article. So a description with a proper name has a definite adjective, just like *Alexander the Great* or *Ivan the Terrible* in English. Read and write:

مصر الحديثة مصر الحديثة **(al-ḥadītha)** *modern Egypt* (f.)

Exercise 1 Make as many meaningful descriptions as possible, using a noun from list (a) and an adjective (making it agree) from list (b). Read and translate your descriptions:

(a) الإعلان، صحيفة، بلاد ، الصورة، رسالة

(b) هامّ، مفيد، شخصي، طويل، محلّي، جميل

Exercise 2 Read and translate these newspaper headings. Which descriptions are masculine, and which feminine? Definite or indefinite?

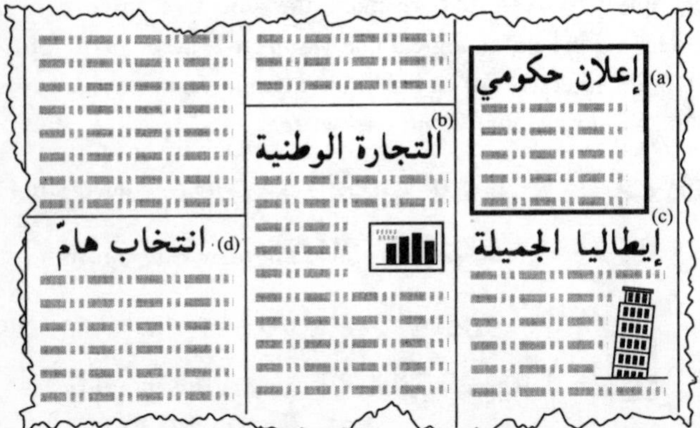

The answers to these exercises follow paragraph 5 below.

3 So far all the descriptions have been singular. Descriptions can also
be dual (though by their nature these are rare). The adjective agrees,
forming its dual in the same manner as the noun. The description can be
indefinite or definite. *Read and write:*

مقرّرين غربيين مقرّرين غربيين
مقرّران غربيان مقرّران غربيان } *two western reporters* (m.)

الرّسالتين الرّسميتين الرّسالتين الرّسميتين ar-risālatayn
ar-rasmīyatayn *both (the) official letters* (f.)

الرّسالتان الرّسميتان (also الرّسالتان الرّسميتان ar-risālatān ar-rasmīyatān)

4 As you would expect, plural descriptions, both indefinite and
definite, also exist. They occur very frequently.

In a plural description, the noun forms its plural in one of the three ways
we have studied in Unit 7 (feminine regular, masculine regular, and the
irregular forms).

But the adjective forms its plural in one of these three ways *only when it
describes people.* We call this the **animate plural** form.

When the adjective describes any other plural noun (animals, things,
places, ideas) it always has the same form as the *feminine singular,*
irrespective of whether the noun is masculine or feminine. We call this
the **inanimate plural** form.

This is a most important rule, and you will see it in action countless times.

Inanimate Plural Rule: *An adjective describing a plural noun
which denotes anything other than people is put into the inanimate
plural form, which is always the same as the feminine singular.*

Read and write these plural descriptions; note the form of the adjective
in each case (an. = animate, inan. = inanimate):

زملاء ممتازين\ون زملاء ممتازين (...ون) zumalā' mumtāzīn (-ūn)

زميلات ممتازات   زميلات ممتازات zamīlāt mumtāzāt
excellent colleagues (f. an. pl.)

افتراحات ممتازه اقتراحات ممتازة **iqtirāḥāt mumtāza**
excellent proposals (inan. pl.)

مقالات ممتازه مقالات ممتازة **maqālāt mumtāza**
excellent articles (inan. pl.)

Remember that the choice between animate pl. and inanimate pl. (= f. sing.) forms arises only for the *adjective*, not the noun. And then only for the *plural*, not the singular or the dual.

Here are more plural descriptions, of various kinds, including a mixture of definite and indefinite (but remember that, since Arabic uses the article for any noun used to cover a whole category in general, you may not always want to express the article in English). Spot the animate plural and inanimate plural adjectives too. Read and write:

بلدان غربيه بلدان غربية **(buldān)** *western countries*

صور ملوّنه صور ملوّنة **ṣuwar mulawwana**
colour(ed) photographs

ممثّلين اجانب ممثلين أجانب **(ajānib)**
foreign representatives

الصحف الأجنبيه الصحف الأجنبية **aṣ-ṣuḥuf al-'ajnabīya**
(the) foreign newspapers

الكمبوترات اليابانيه الكمبيوترات اليابانية
(the) Japanese computers

مندوبين يابانيين مندوبين يابانيين **(mandūbīn)**
Japanese delegates

اعلانات حكوميه إعلانات حكومية
government announcements

زميلات مجتهدات زميلات مجتهدات **(mujtahidāt)**
hard-working colleagues (f.)

Possessive

5 In English the so-called *possessive* (more correctly, possessive adjective) is a word: *my, your, his, her, its, our, your, their*. In Arabic it is an ending added to the word denoting what is possessed. Write *colleague* in Arabic, indefinite masculine form:

زميل زميل

Now add the ending ...ـي -ī and you get *my colleague* (m.):

زميلي زميلي **zamīlī**

A final ة on the possessed noun changes to ت (since ة can stand only at the end of a word) before the possessive ending is added. Write *my car*:

سيّارتي سيّارتي **sayyāratī**

Here are the possessive endings for all the persons we need, including *my* which we have just studied:

...ـي	**-ī**	*my*	...نا	**-na**	*our*
...ك	**-ak**	*your* (m.)	...كم	**-kum**	*your* (pl.)
...ك	**-ik**	*your* (f.)			
...ه	**-u, -hu**	*his, its* (m.)	...ـهم	**-hum**	*their* (animate pl.)
...ـها	**-ha**	*her, its* (f.), *their* (inanimate pl.)			

These are all added to the indefinite noun in the same way as ...ـي .
Read and write:

تقريري تقريري **taqrīrī** *my report*

مشكلتي مشكلتي **mu<u>sh</u>kilatī** *my problem*

اقتراحك اقتراحك **iqtirāḥak, …ik** *your proposal*

لجنتك لجنتك **lajnatak, …ik** *your committee*

مكتبه مكتبه **maktabu** *his office*

صورته صورته **ṣūratu** *his, its picture*

اسمها اسمها **ismhā** *her, its, their* (inan.) *name*

احتجاجنا احتجاجنا **iḥtijājna** *our objection*

مجلّتنا مجلّتنا **majallatna** *our magazine*

وصولكم وصولكم **wusūlkum** *your* (pl.) *arrival*

زيارتكم زيارتكم **ziyāratkum** *your* (pl.) *visit*

اعلانهم إعلانهم **i9lānhum** *their advertisement*

طائرتهم طائرتهم **ṭā'irathum** *their aeroplane*

Certain things need explaining:

- The possessive *you* shown above has three forms: one used when the 'possessor' is a male person, one used when the possessor is a female person, and one used when the possessors constitute a group.
- We use the possessive **-u** or **-hu** when the possessor would be expressed with a masculine noun; we have to translate with *his* or *its* as appropriate.
- We use the possessive **-ha** when the possessor would be expressed with a feminine noun, *or a plural noun not denoting people* (this is the inanimate plural again); we have to translate with *her*, *its* or *their* as appropriate.
- We use the possessive **-hum** *their* only when the possessors are people, i.e. animate.
- No dual? Yes, there are dual possessives (= *of you both*, *of them both*), but they are so rarely used that we need not learn them, and they have been left out of this table.

When a noun has a possessive ending attached, it logically becomes definite. So any accompanying adjective has the article. Read and write:

مكتبي الجديد مكتبي الجديد **maktabī l-jadīd**
my new office

لزيارتك الرسمية لزيارتك الرسمية **li-ziyāratak ar-rasmīya**
for your official visit

منظّمته الصغيره منظمته الصغيرة **munaẓẓamatu ṣ-ṣaghīra**
his small organisation

انتاجهم الصناعي إنتاجهم الصناعي **intājhum aṣ-ṣinā9ī**
their industrial production

We can also add these possessives to a noun with the regular plural noun ending ات..., or to an irregular plural. ***Read and write:***

معلوماتهم المفيدة معلوماتهم المفيده **ma9lūmāthum al-mufīda**
their useful information
مشاكلنا الفنّية مشاكلنا الفنيّة **ma<u>sh</u>ākilna l-fannīya**
our technical problems

Adding a possessive to a noun with the dual ending, or with the regular plurals ...ين\...ون **-īn/ūn**, involves various changes which are frankly not worth our trouble, since these forms are very rarely found with possessives. We can ignore them.

Exercise 3 Who placed advertisement (a)? And what is the firm which placed advertisement (b) looking for? (Read only the big print!):

(b)

(a)

Exercise 4 Read and translate the following descriptions:

(a) صور ملوّنة (b) للمقرّرين الأجانب (c) منظّمتنا الفنّية
(d) الصحافة المحلّية والوطنية (e) مكتبك الجديد

The answers to these exercises are given immediately below.

Answers to Exercises

Exercise 1

الإعلان الهامّ\المفيد\الشخصي\الطويل\المحلّي\الجميل **al-'i9lān al-hāmm, al-mufīd, a<u>sh</u>-<u>sh</u>a<u>kh</u>ṣī, aṭ-ṭawīl, al-maḥallī, al-jamīl**
the important, useful, personal, long, local, beautiful announcement/advertisement

صحيفة هامّة\مفيدة\محلّية **ṣaḥīfa hāmma, mufīda, maḥallīya**
an important, a useful, local newspaper

بلاد هامّ\جميل **bilad hāmm, jamīl** *an important, a beautiful country*

الصورة الهامّة\المفيدة\الشخصية\الجميلة **aṣ-ṣūra l-hāmma, l-mufīda, <u>sh</u>-<u>sh</u>a<u>kh</u>ṣīya, l-jamīla** *the important, useful, personal (private), beautiful picture/photograph*

رسالة هامّة\مفيدة\شخصية\طويلة\جميلة **risāla hāmma, mufīda, shakhṣīya, ṭawīla, jamīla** *an important, a useful, private, long, beautiful letter*

Exercise 2 (a) **i9lān ḥukūmī** *Government(al) Announcement/Notice*, indefinite masculine

(b) **at-tijāra l-waṭanī** *('The') National Trade*, definite feminine

(c) **īṭāliya l-jamīla** *Beautiful Italy ('Italy the Beautiful')*, definite feminine

(d) **intikhāb hāmm** *an important election*, indefinite masculine

Exercise 3 (a) **al-khuṭūṭ al-jawwīya l-waṭanīya** *('The') National Airlines ('Air Lines')*

(b) **mumaththilīn fannīyīn** *Technical Representatives*

Exercise 4 (a) **ṣuwar mulawwana** *coloured pictures/photographs*

(b) **li-l-muqarrirīn al-'ajānib** *for ('the') foreign reporters*

(c) **munaẓẓamatna l-fannīya** *our technical organisation*

(d) **aṣ-ṣiḥāfa l-maḥallīya wa l-waṭanīya** *the local and national press*

(e) **maktabak al-jadīd** *your new office*

Tests

1 Read aloud and translate:

(a) صحافتنا الأسبوعية
(b) احتجاجاتهم الطّويلة
(c) الزّملاء الفنّيين
(d) صحف عربية
(e) بنك أجنبي

2 Put adjective and noun together in a description, changing the adjective as necessary:

(a) مدرسة، ابتدائي
(b) المطر، وطني
(c) تقاريره، يومي
(d) لزوّارنا، أجنبي
(e) انتخابات، عامّ

3 Make these descriptions plural:

(a) رسالة طويلة
(b) التقرير الفنّي
(c) ممثّل أجنبي
(d) الطائرة الأميركية
(e) خطّ جوّي

Review

An important step. Once you have mastered this unit, you have broken through the barrier separating single words from meaningful expressions. And you have done your first manipulations in the language.

The words are hard, and there are too many to remember at a first attempt. Concentrate on the essential vocabulary; but don't hesitate to look up any word at all if you are uncertain.

10

In this unit you will learn

- the personal pronouns,
- the second basic structure, making simple statements.

New Words: العمل al-9amal *Work*

1 *Essential Vocabulary*

تاجر تجّار	**tājir tujjār** *trader*	مأمور	**ma'mūr** *public official*
خبير خبراء	**khabīr khubarā'** *expert*	مدني	**madanī** *civil, urban*
دولي	**duwalī** *international*	مشهور	**mashhūr** *famous*
صعب صعاب	**ṣa9b ṣi9āb** *difficult*	مهندس	**muhandis** *engineer*
طبيب أطبّاء	**ṭabīb aṭibbā'** *doctor*	موجود	**moujūd** *present* (not absent)
عالمي	**9ālamī** *world(wide)*	موظّف	**muwaẓẓaf** *employee*
غائب	**ghā'ib** *absent*	وكالة	**wikāla** *agency*

Reference Vocabulary

أجر أجور	**ajr ujūr** *wage*	ممرّض\ممرّضة	**mumarriḍ(a)** *nurse*
بطالة	**baṭāla** *unemployment*	هندسة	**handasa** *engineering*
راتب رواتب	**rātib rawātib** *salary*	واضح	**wāḍiḥ** *clear*
سمسار سماسير	**simsār samāsīr** *broker*	وظيفة وظائف	**waẓīfa waẓā'if** *job, post*
شغل أشغال	**shughl ashghāl** *work, job*	وكيل وكلاء	**wakīl wukalā'** *agent*
عمل أعمال	**9amal a9māl** *work, labour*		
معقول	**ma9qūl** *reasonable*		
مقبول	**maqbūl** *acceptable*		

Personal pronouns

2 In previous units we have seen most of the personal pronouns ('I, you, he' etc.) . It may be helpful to have them clearly set out, with one we haven't seen so far. Write them out:

انا أنا **ana** *I* — نحن نحن **naḥnu** *we*

انت أنت **anta** *you* (m.) — انتم أنتم **antum** *you* (pl.)

انت أنت **anti** *you* (f.)

هو هو **huwa** *he, it* (m.) — هم هم **hum** *they* (people)

هي هي **hiya** *she, it,* (f.), *they* (other than people, i.e. inanimate pl.)

These pronouns correspond exactly to the possessives given in Unit 9, paragraph 5. The notes given there apply here as well.

Basic Structures, 2: The Equation

3 You probably didn't realise that you can already read and write whole sentences in Arabic. Well, you can. ***Read and write*** these ones:

هو مسؤول . هو مسؤول. **(mas'ūl)**
He is responsible.

هو مهندس . هو مهندس. **(muhandis)**
He is an engineer.

زميله مسؤول . زميله مسؤول. **(zamīlu)**
His colleague is responsible.

زميله طبيب . زميله طبيب.
His colleague is a doctor.

زميله صحفي مصري . زميله صحفي مصري. *His colleague is an Egyptian journalist.*

It is as simple as that. Whereas in English we need a verb form 'is' for such a sentence, Arabic needs nothing beyond the two parts of the statement. These Arabic sentences are complete and correct.

(English uses this verbless structure also, but only in newspaper headlines and the like: *"Dollar Devalued"*, *"Chairman Dismissed"*, *"Farmers Furious"*.)

We can call this structure an **equation**, because, like a mathematical equation such as *'x = 2'*, both parts are regarded as equal to each other. The equation is the second of the three basic structures which we study. We can use any pronoun in the first part of the equation.

Read and write:

انا مسؤول . أنا مسؤول. *I am responsible.*

هي مسؤولة. — هي مسؤوله. *She is responsible.*

هي طبيبة مشهورة. — هي طبيبه مشهوره. **(mashhūra)** *She is a famous doctor.*

> **Equation Rule:** *In a simple statement, Arabic does not use any verb form corresponding to the English 'am, is, are'. The verb is simply omitted.*

You will notice that the second part has to agree with the first part. Also, we can of course have a noun instead of a pronoun. For both, we observe the *inanimate plural rule* (Unit 9, paragraph 4) throughout. ***Read and write***, with an eye on the inanimate plural:

المشكلة صعبة. — المشكله صعبه. **(ṣa9ba)** *The problem is difficult.* (feminine singular)

المشاكل صعبة — المشاكل صعبه. *The problems are difficult.* (inanimate plural)

الاقتراحات طويلة. — الاقتراحات طويله. **(al-iqtirāḥāt)** *The proposals are long.*

هي طويلة. — هي طويله. **hiya ṭawīla.** *They (the proposals) are long.*

When we have to use a masculine regular plural ending in an equation, it takes the form **...ون -ūn** (not **...ين -īn**); when we use a dual, it takes the form **...ان -ān** (not **...ين -ayn**). ***Read and write:***

المفتّشون مسؤولون. — المفتّشون مسؤولون. *The inspectors are responsible.*

المفتّشان مسؤولان. — المفتّشان مسؤولان. *Both inspectors are responsible.*

نحن مسرورون. — نحن مسرورون. **(masrūrūn)** *We are pleased.*

Exercise 1 Make as many meaningful equations as possible, taking your first part from list (a) and your second part from list (b). The words must be used as they are; don't change their form:

(a) اقتراحاتنا ، هي ، الرئيس، المندوبون، الصحفي

(b) موجودون، مقبولة، موجود ، واضحة، عراقي

Exercise 2 Translate into Arabic and read your answer aloud:

(a) *The engineer is Lebanese.* (b) *They are Italians.*
(c) *The minister is absent.* (d) *The doctor is German.*
(e) *She is a foreign doctor.*

The answers to these exercises follow paragraph 4 below.

We have said that the second part of the equation must agree with the first part. This is only partly true. Look back at the equations quoted so far, especially the ones beginning with a noun. Can you see any way in which the second part does *not* agree with the first part?

Here is a clue. ***Read and write*** this expression, which bears some resemblance to one of the equations we have already written:

المشكلة الصعبة المشكلة الصعبة **al-mushkila ṣ-ṣa9ba**

You see the difference. What we have here is not an equation at all, but a *description* (Unit 9): '*the difficult problem*'. In a description the adjective agrees with the noun in every possible way, including indefinite/definite. The equations we have written earlier in this paragraph have a definite first part but an *indefinite* second part.

We can have equations with a definite second part. But they almost always have a pronoun in the first part. ***Read and write:***

هو الرئيس. هو الرئيس. **(ar-ra'īs)** *He is the chairman.*

هم الخبراء. هم الخبراء. *They are the experts.*

If the meaning of the equation demands a noun in the first part, then we use the noun but we re-state it with its corresponding pronoun.
Read and write:

العراقي هو الرئيس. العراقي هو الرئيس. *The Iraqi ('he') is the chairman.*

زملائي هم الخبراء. زملائي هم الخبراء. *My colleagues ('they') are the experts.*

Adding the pronoun makes it impossible to read the expression as a description. It must be an equation. But such equations are comparatively rare. Equations of the type we have studied earlier in the paragraph, with an *indefinite* second part, are much more common.

4 Equations with descriptions

Either part of an equation can itself be a description. As long as the relationship between the two parts is respected, the equation is still correct. Look back at the fifth and eighth examples in paragraph 3 above:

زميله صحفي مصري.　　　　هي طبيبة مشهورة.

in which the second part consists of a description. We can have the first part as a description; or indeed both parts. If the equation begins to look a little heavy or complicated, the writer may break it up by adding the corresponding pronoun to the first part, showing clearly which part is which. We can always do this, with any equation. ***Read and write:***

المهندس المدني موجود.
al-muhandis al-mădanī moujūd.
The civil engineer is present.

المهندس المدني موجود.

المندوب العربي هو مهندس مدني.
The Arab delegate ('he') is a civil engineer.

المندوب العربي هو مهندس مدني.

Exercise 3 Read and translate these newspaper headings; then answer the questions:

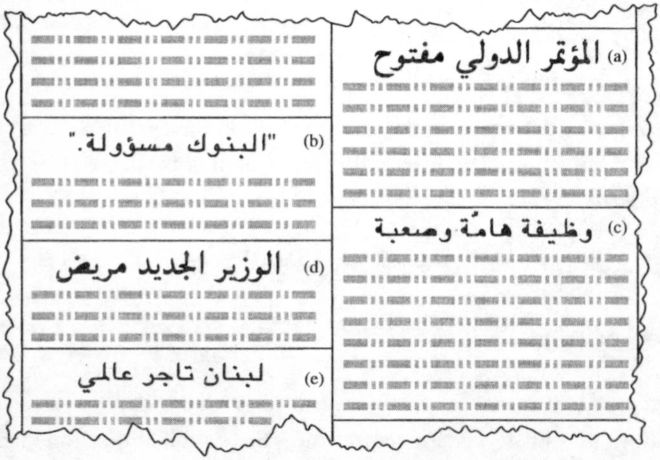
(a) المؤتمر الدولي مفتوح
(b) "البنوك مسؤولة."
(c) وظيفة هامّة وصعبة
(d) الوزير الجديد مريض
(e) لبنان تاجر عالمي

Which ones are equations and which are descriptions? Which equations (if any) contain a description?

Exercise 4 Read aloud and translate:

(a) الطبيب إنجليزي. (b) الاقتراحات معقولة.

(c) هو خبير فنّي. (d) مصر كبيرة.

(e) اقتراحنا جديد.

The answers to these exercises are given immediately below.

Answers to Exercises

Exercise 1 اقتراحتنا مقبولة\واضحة. **iqtirāḥātna maqbūla/wāḍiḥa.**

Our proposals are acceptable/clear.

هي مقبولة\واضحة. **hiya maqbula/wāḍiḥa.**

It is / They are acceptable/clear.

الرّئيس موجود\عراقي. **ar-ra'īs moujūd /9irāqī.**

The chairman is present /Iraqi.

المندوبون موجودون. **al-mandūbūn moujūdūn.**

The delegates are present.

الصحفي موجود\عراقي. **aṣ-ṣuḥufī moujūd /9irāqī.**

The journalist is present /Iraqi.

Exercise 2 (a) المهندس لبناني. **al-muhandis lubnānī.**

(b) هم إطاليون. **hum īṭālīyūn.** (c) الوزير غائب. **al-wazīr gh̲ā'ib.**

(d) الطّبيب ألماني. **aṭ-ṭabīb almānī.**

(e) هي طبيبة أجنبية. **hiya ṭabība ajnabīya.**

Exercise 3 (a) **al-mu'tamar ad-duwalī maftūḥ.** *The international conference is open.* Equation with a definite description as first part.

(b) **al-bunūk mas'ūla.** *The banks are responsible.* Equation.

(c) **waẓīfa hāmma wa-ṣa9ba** *An important and difficult job.* Not an equation but an indefinite description.

(d) **al-wazīr al-jadīd marīḍ.** *The new minister is ill.* Equation with a definite description as first part.

(e) **lubnān tājir 9ālamī.** *Lebanon is a world trader.* Equation with an indefinite description as second part.

Exercise 4 (a) **aṭ-ṭabīb ingilīzī.** *The doctor is British/English.*
(b) **al-iqtirāḥāt ma9qūla**. *The proposals are reasonable.*
(c) **huwa <u>kh</u>abīr fannī.** *He is a technical expert.*
(d) **miṣr kabīra.** *Egypt is big.*
(e) **iqtirāḥna jadīd.** *Our proposal is new.*

Tests

1 Read aloud and translate:

(a) وظيفته صعبة. (b) المؤتمر التجاري هامّ.
(c) الوزراء موجودون. (d) الصورة جميلة.
(e) الصورة الجميلة

2 Put the words together in an equation, making any necessary changes. Read aloud your answer and translate it:

(a) موظّفون؛ مسرور. (b) مطارنا، دولي؛ هامّ.
(c) هو؛ تاجر، دولي. (d) النصّ؛ واضح، ومقبول.
(e) مأمور؛ مشغول.

3 Fill in the missing letter. Read aloud and translate the word:

(a) و...يفة (b) مـ...ظّف (c) مـ..دوب
(d) غا...ب (e) الخـ..راء

Review

With an understanding of *descriptions* studied in the last unit and *equations* studied in this unit, you have made a serious step towards being able to read and understand the headings of many notices and announcements, and many newspaper headlines. There remains a third basic structure, also related to these two. But before we tackle that one, we should arm ourselves with some important prepositions (*to, from, in, with* and the like), which come in the next unit.

11

In this unit you will learn

- important prepositions,
- the command form of the verb,
- a form of equation often used in signs.

New Words: البلد al-balad *Town*

1 *Essential Vocabulary - Prepositions*

إلى	**ila** *to*	في	**fī** *in*
ب	**bi-** *with, by, in*	قبل	**qabl** *before*
بعد	**ba9d** *after*	ل	**li-** *to, for, of*
على	**9ala** *on*	مع	**ma9** *with*
عن	**9an** *from, about*	من	**min** *from*

Essential Vocabulary - Other words

إشارة	**ishāra** *sign*	مرور	**murūr**(also:) *passing, turning*
إيقاف	**īqāf** *parking*		
بلد بلاد	**balad bilād** *town*	مفرق مفارق	**mafraq mafāriq** *crossroad*
بوليس	**būlīs** *police*		
تدخين	**tadkhīn** *smoking*	ممنوع	**mamnū9** *prohibited*
توقيف	**touqīf** *parking*	ميدان ميادين	**maydān mayādīn** *square*
حدّ حدود	**ḥadd ḥudūd** *limit*		
سرعة	**sur9a** *speed*	نقل	**naql** *transport*
طريق طرق	**ṭarīq ṭuruq** *road*	وقوف	**wuqūf** *stopping*
كراج\جراج	**garāj** *garage*	يسار	**yasār** *left(-hand)*
كيلومتر\كم	**kīlomitr** *kilometre*	يمين	**yamīn** *right(-hand)*
مدينة مدن	**madīna mudun** *city*		

Reference Vocabulary - Prepositions

أمام	**amām** *in front of*	خلال	**khilāl** *during*
تحت	**taḥt** *below, under*	داخل	**dākhil** *inside*
حسب	**ḥasab** *according to*	دون\بدون	**dūn, bidūn** *without*
خارج	**khārij** *outside*	ضدّ	**ḍidd** *against*

غير **ghayr** *apart from* — ك\مثل **ka-, mithl** *like, as*

فوق **fouq** *above, over* — وراء **warā'** *behind, beyond*

Reference Vocabulary - Other words

برلمان **barlamān** *parliament* — قصر قصور **qaṣr qusūr** *palace*

بلدية **baladīya** *town hall* — قنصلية **qunṣulīya** *consulate*

جامعة **jāmi9a** *university* — مجلس مجالس **majlis majālis** *council*

شرطي **shurṭī** *policeman* — مركز مراكز **markaz marākiz** *centre*

عاصمة عواصم **9āṣima 9awāṣim** *capital city*

2 Prepositions

A preposition is a word connecting a noun or pronoun with the rest of the sentence. Examples in English are *in, with, from*. In the essential and reference vocabularies given above the prepositions are shown separately because of their importance.

In Arabic the preposition precedes its noun, as it does in English. ***Read and write:***

بعد سنة — بعد سنة **ba9d sana** *after a year*

ضدّ الحكومة — ضدّ الحكومة **(ḍidd)** *against the government*

حسب الخبراء — حسب الخبراء **(ḥasab)** *according to the experts*

داخل البلاد — داخل البلاد **(dākhil)** *inside the country*

في **fī** shortens its vowel, becoming **fi** in pronunciation before an article. The spelling is unchanged. ***Read and write***, comparing the sounds:

في بنك — في بنك **fī bank** *in a bank* (long **ī**)

في البنك — في البنك **fi l-bank** *in the bank* (short **i**)

When we want to combine a preposition with a *pronoun*, we add the pronoun as an ending, using the same endings as the possessives (Unit 9, paragraph 5). The meanings then become *me, you, him* etc. We can add the pronoun endings to the prepositions which end in a consonant (including **hamza**) without further ado. ***Read and write:***

معي معي **ma9ī** *with me* أمامه امامه **amāmu** *in front of him*

The prepositions ending in a vowel, long or short, are unfortunately not so simple. Details are given below. Don't try to learn the following details at one stroke. Use them for reference until at least some become familiar. Some of the explanation concerns only pronunciation anyway, which is not our main target.

- إلى **ila** and على **9ala** change to ...إليـ **ilay-** and ...عليـ **9alay-** before adding a pronoun. ***Read and write:***

  اليها إليها **ilayha** *to her, it, them* (inanimate pl.)

  علينا علينا **alayna** *up to us ('on us')*

  You have certainly heard of the classic greeting السّلام عليكم **as-salām 9alaykum** *Peace (be) upon you.* Thinking of this might help you to remember how these two prepositions change before a pronoun.

- ل **li-** (you will recall that one-letter words are written together with the next word) becomes لي **lī** for 'for me', but changes to **la-** before any other pronoun. ***Read and write:***

  له له **lahu** *for him, it* لهم لهم **lahum** *for them*

- After ب **bi-**, ...إليـ **ilay-** and ...عليـ **9alay-** (see above), the pronoun ending ...ه is pronounced **-hi**, and ...هم is pronounced **-him**. The spelling is unchanged. ***Read and write:***

  به به **bihi** *with him/it, in him/it* اليهم إليهم **ilayhim** *to them*

3 Prepositions in Equations

We can use a phrase consisting of preposition + noun, or preposition + pronoun, as either part of an equation, without further formality.

Read and write:

هو ضدّ الاقتراح. هو ضدّ الاقتراح. هو ضدّ الاقتراح. *He is against the proposal.*

الطبيب في البلد. الطبيب في البلد. * الطبيب في البلد. *The doctor is in ('the') town.*

المرور إلى اليسار ممنوع. المرور الى اليسار ممنوع.

al-murur ila l-yasār mamnū9.

NO LEFT TURN (*'Turning left prohibited'*)

* No 'helping' pronoun (Unit 10, paragraph 3) is needed here. The preposition makes the equation clear and unmistakable.

4 Translating prepositions

Arabic phrases do not always have the preposition which exactly corresponds to the English; be prepared for different ones. Here are two examples out of many. ***Read and write:***

مسؤول عن مسؤول عن **(9an)** *responsible for*

ممنون من ممنون من **(min)** *grateful for*

5 Command Form

You may see a notice or instruction like one of these. ***Read and write:***

اشرب فانتا اشرب فانتا **ishrab fanta** *Drink Fanta*

اقفل الباب اقفل الباب **(iqfil)** *Shut the Door*

اركب\انزل هنا اركب\انزل هنا **irkab/inzil huna** *Get on/off here*

افتح بانتباه افتح بانتباه **iftaḥ bi-ntibāh** *Open carefully*

انظر ... انظر.. **unẓur** *See ...*

اطلب ... اطلب... **uṭlub** *Ask for ...*

These are verbs, in the command form. They can often be recognised by two characteristics: they stand at the beginning of the expression, as in English; and they begin with **alif**, which is pronounced **i-**, **u-** or **a-** depending on the verb.

Unfortunately not all commands take this easily recognisable form. In Unit 3 we had **تمهّل tamahhal** *SLOW DOWN*, and in Unit 6 **قف qif** *STOP*. These important notices are also in the command form.

All the forms shown here are masculine, which is the form generally used;

you may occasionally see the plural form (as if addressing a group), which adds ...وا pronounced **-ū** (the **alif** is silent):

اشربوا **ishrabū** *Drink;* **...** اطلبوا **uṭlubū** *Ask for* ... (etc.)

These forms are used in advertisements, or when an authoritative tone (police, road signs, warnings of danger etc.) is needed. A more polite form, similar to our *Please* ... takes the following guise. ***Read and write:***

الرجاء الانتظار هنا. الرجاء الانتظار هنا. **ar-rajā’ al-intiẓar huna.** *Please Wait Here.*

You will note that the verbal noun, in this case انتظار *waiting*, is definite in this expression.

Please do not ... is written using the noun عدم **9adam** *lack of*, followed by a definite verbal noun. ***Read and write:***

الرجاء عدم التّدخين. الرجاء عدم التدخين. **ar-rajā’ 9adam at-tadkhīn.** *Please do not Smoke.*

6 Signs and Notices

In many road signs and similar short messages and warnings, an equation is used in reverse order, for effect. This happens, for example, with the essential word ممنوع **mamnū9** *PROHIBITED*. In an ordinary text, the sentence *Entry is prohibited* would be

الدخول ممنوع. **ad-dukhūl mamnu9.**

This is the normal word-order for an equation, as you have learned. But often the same sentence in a sign will read

ممنوع الدخول *NO ENTRY (‘Entry prohibited’)*

for special effect. Don’t be surprised when you see this. It is simply an equation with its parts in reverse order.

Not all Arab countries use the same words for everything, so don’t be confused if you find unfamiliar words on traffic and other signs. The words given in this book are very widely used.

Exercise 1 Read and translate these equations:

(a) الاسم فوق الإعلان.   (b) المفرق خارج البلد.

(c) مكتبي أمام المستشفى.   (d) الكراج على يمينك.

(e) البلدية وراءنا.

Exercise 2 Write equations with the opposite meaning of those shown in Exercise 2. Read your answers aloud.

Exercise 3 Fit the captions to the signs, one of which we know already. Read the captions aloud and translate them:

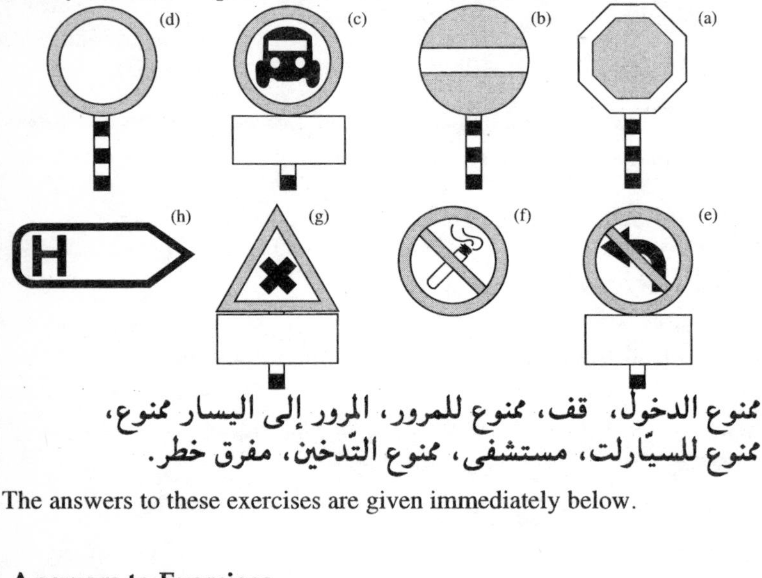

ممنوع الدخول، قف، ممنوع للمرور، المرور إلى اليسار ممنوع، ممنوع للسيّارلت، مستشفى، ممنوع التّدخين، مفرق خطر.

The answers to these exercises are given immediately below.

Answers to Exercises

Exercise 1 (a) al-ism fouq al-'i9lān.

The name is above the announcement.

(b) **al-mafraq <u>kh</u>ārij al-balad.** *The crossroad is outside the town.*

(c) **maktabī amām al-musta<u>sh</u>fa.** *My office is in front of the hospital.*

(d) **al-garāj 9ala yamīnak.** *The garage is on your right.*

(e) **al-baladīya warā'na.** *The town hall is behind us.*

Exercise 2 (a) الاسم نحت الإعلان. al-ism taḥt al-'i9lān.

(b) المفرق داخل البلد. al-mafraq dā<u>kh</u>il al-balad.

(c) مكتبي وراء المستشفى. maktabī warā' al-musta<u>sh</u>fa.

(d) الكراج علي يسارك. al-garāj 9ala yasārak.
(e) البلدية أمامنا. al-baladīya amāmna.

Exercise 3 (a) قف **qif** *STOP*
(b) ممنوع الدخول **mamnū9 ad-dukhūl** *NO ENTRY*
(c) ممنوع للسيّارلت **mamnū9 li-s-sayyārāt** *VEHICLES PROHIBITED*
(d) ممنوع للمرور **mamnū9 li-l-murūr** *TRAFFIC PROHIBITED*
(e) المرور إلى اليسار ممنوع **al-murūr ila l-yasār mamnū9** *NO LEFT TURN*
(f) ممنوع التّدخين **mamnū9 at-tadkhīn** *NO SMOKING*
(g) مفرق خطر **mafraq khaṭir** *DANGEROUS CROSSROAD*
(h) مستشفى **mustashfa** *HOSPITAL*

Tests

1 Read aloud and translate:

(a) ممنوع الانتظار (b) في البلد (c) في البلاد*
(d) أشغال على الطريق (e) المرور إلى اليمين

* two possible meanings

2 Make the adjective agree with the noun or pronoun in a description:

(a) سيّارات (جديد) (b) أشغال (هامّ)
(c) الشرطة (محلّي) (d) مستشفيات (كبير)
(e) مشاكل (فنّي)

3 Which of these are descriptions, and which are equations? (All full stops have been omitted, not to make things too easy.) Read everything aloud and translate it:

(a) المأمور المسؤول (b) المأمورون هم المسؤولون
(c) البلاد جميل (d) زميلي في المستشفى
(e) زميلي المريض

Review

Prepositions are useful because of their function in linking words, opening up phrases which otherwise might be a problem. They are so common that they are not only worth learning; they stick in the mind more easily than many other words. And they fit into the equation structure which is at the heart of many headlines and announcements.

We go on now to our third and last basic structure.

12

In this unit you will learn

- the third basic structure, linking two or more nouns.

New Words: الإدارة al-'idāra *Administration*

1 *Essential Vocabulary*

تأمين **ta'mīn** *insurance*

تسجيل **tasjīl** *registration*

جمرك **jumruk** *customs*

حساب **ḥisāb** *account*

دائرة دوائر **dā'ira dawā'ir** *directorate*

دفع مدفوعات **daf9 madfū9āt** *payment*

رخصة رخص **ru<u>kh</u>ṣa ru<u>kh</u>aṣ** *licence*

ضريبة ضرائب **ḍarība ḍarā'ib** *tax*

عقد عقود **9aqd 9uqūd** *contract*

قسم أقسام **qism aqsām** *department*

نمرة نمر **numra numar** *number*

اليوم **al-youm** *today*

Reference Vocabulary

اقتصاد **iqtiṣād** *economy, economics*

تربية **tarbiya** *education*

خارجية **<u>kh</u>ārijīya** *Foreign Affairs*

داخلية **dā<u>kh</u>ilīya** *Home Affairs*

دفاع **difā9** *defence*

زراعة **zirā9a** *agriculture*

سياسة **siyāsa** *policy, politics*

مالية **mālīya** *Financial Affairs*

نفط **nafṭ** *oil*

Basic Structures, 3: The Construct

2 Write the two nouns

مكتب مكتب *an office*

المدير المدير *the manager*

Now put these two together as they stand, and you have:

مكتب المدير مكتب المدير **maktab al-mudīr** *the manager's office*

Now *read and write:*

الشركة الشركة *the company*

Now ***read and write*** *the company office* or *the company's office*:

مكتب الشركة مكتب الشركة مكتب الشركة **maktab ash-sharika**

Now ***read and write*** these expressions, which are exactly similar in form:

بيت المدير بيت المدير *the manager's house*

عقد العمّال عقد العمّال **(9aqd)** *the workers' contract*

شغل زميلي شغل زميلي *my colleague's work*

تسجيل السيّارات * تسجيل السيّارات **(tasjīl)** *car ('cars') registration*

طريق المطار طريق المطار **ṭarīq al-maṭār** *the airport road*

Simply by putting two nouns together, with no other words at all, we build an association between them. The nature of this association is often possession, but not always.

This type of expression is our third basic structure; it is called a **construct**. We have to observe two simple rules in making a construct:

- the *qualifying* noun (**مدير**) follows the *qualified* noun (**مكتب**); think of the word-order of *the leg of the table*; so: *the office of the manager*.
- only the last noun can have a definite 'marker', i.e. either the article **..الـ** (Units 2 and 3) or a possessive ending (Unit 9); the first noun must remain *indefinite* in form.

* Remember (Unit 2) that when a noun is used generally or universally ('cars'), Arabic makes it definite, unlike English.

> **Construct Rule 1:** *In a construct, only the last noun can have the article or a possessive ending.*

Now ***read and write*** a couple of constructs with a proper name as last noun:

مكتب احمد مكتب احمد **(aḥmad)** *Aḥmad's office*

اقتصاد مصر اقتصاد مصر **(iqtiṣād)** *the economy of Egypt*

These are still correct: the first noun is indefinite in form, and the last noun is definite because it is a proper noun or name, which is definite by nature.

Exercise 1 Read aloud and translate the following nameplates, which are all in the form of constructs:

(a) قسم الحسابات (b) مدخل الوزارة (c) مدير المكتب

(d) قسم التسجيل (e) استقبال الزوار (f) مكتب المدفوعات

Exercise 2 Put each pair into a construct. Read it out and translate it:

(a) مكتب، عقود (b) قسم، هندسة (c) تأمين، بيتي (d) شغل، وزارة

Exercise 3 Which way, right or left, to (a) *Traffic Department* (b) *Tax Office* (c) *Car Registration* (d) *Issue of Licences*?

Read each direction aloud:

→ قسم المرور ← تسجيل السيّارات

→ إصدار الرخص ← مكتب الضرائب

The answers to these exercises follow paragraph 7 below.

When the first noun of a construct ends in ة... , this is pronounced **-at**. In handwriting we always write the dots of ة here. Write the word for *ministry*:

وزارة وزارة

Now ***read and write*** *Ministry of Labour*, and note the pronunciation of the first noun:

وزارة العمل وزارة العمل **wizāra*t* al-9amal**

Now write the same construct, but replacing *Labour* with *Economy*, *Foreign Affairs* and *Agriculture*:

وزارة الاقتصاد وزارة الاقتصاد **wizārat al-iqtiṣād**
Ministry of Economy

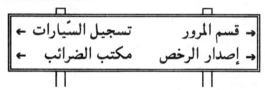

وزارة الخارجيه وزارة الخارجية **wizārat al-khārijīya** *Ministry of Foreign Affairs*

وزارة الزراعه وزارة الزراعة **wizārat az-zirā9a** *Ministry of Agriculture*

You will notice from the last two examples that the pronunciation of **ة...** (if there is one) on the *last* noun does not change. It remains **-a**.

Exercise 4 Write the name of each Ministry:
(a) *Labour* (b) *Education* (c) *Defence* (d) *Agriculture* (e) *Industry*
Read your answers aloud.

Exercise 5 Repeat Exercise 4 with *Directorate* for *Ministry.*

The answers to these exercises are given after paragraph 7 below.

3 Now ***read and write*** the following constructs:

مدير بنك مدير بنك **mudīr bank** *a bank manager*

موظّف شركه موظّف شركة **muwaẓẓaf sharika** *a company employee*

نمرة تلفون نمرة تلفون **numrat tilifōn** *a telephone number*

Do you see the difference? The last noun is now indefinite, making the whole construct indefinite in meaning. Compare definite and indefinite constructs with identical original elements. ***Read and write:***

مدير البنك مدير البنك **mudīr al-bank** *the bank manager*

مدير بنك مدير بنك **mudīr bank** *a bank manager*

Remember that only the last noun, i.e. the qualifier, changes, not the first noun.

You will meet definite constructs far more often than indefinite ones.

Construct Rule 2: *A construct is definite or indefinite according to whether the last noun is definite or indefinite.*

Exercise 6 Make indefinite constructs with these pairs of nouns. Read aloud and translate your answers:

(a) رئيس، وزارة (b) مدير، شركة (c) نمرة، سيّارة (d) تسجيل، عقد

The answers to this exercise follow paragraph 7 below.

4 So much for constructs consisting of two nouns. We also have constructs with more than two nouns. ***Read and write:***

مكتب الضرائب والتسجيل مكتب الضرائب والتسجيل **maktab aḍ-ḍarā'ib wa-t-tasjīl** *Tax and Registration Office*

We can call this one a *compound* construct: it has one first noun and two 'last' or qualifying nouns.

Here is another variant. ***Read and write:***

نمرة تلفون المكتب نمرة تلفون المكتب **numrat tilifōn al-maktab** *the office telephone number*

We can call this one a *string* construct; each noun except the last one is qualified, and made definite, by the next noun.

In these two types, as in all constructs, the two construct rules given in paragraphs 2 and 3 above still apply.

5 Arabic treats the construct as a unit. An adjective is not allowed to interrupt it. Any adjective must follow the whole construct, even if confusion results. ***Read and write:***

نمرة الشركة الجديدة نمرة الشركة الجديدة **numrat ash-sharika l-jadīda** *the company's new number* or *the new company's number*

You will meet the construct, especially the definite two-noun variety (**maktab al-mudīr**, paragraph 2 above) countless times in notices, signs, newspaper headlines and the like.

6 In Unit 3 we learned the important preposition ل **li** *'to, for'*. ل can also mean *of*, and it often allows us to make expressions which have the same meaning as a construct, but avoiding its constraints. With ل we can use the article, adjectives etc. for example, just as we wish. **Read and write** these constructs, already familiar to you:

مدير البنك   مدير البنك

نمرة الشركة   نمرة الشركة

نمرة تلفون المكتب   نمره تلغون المكتب

نمرة الشركة الجديدة   نمرة الشرك الجديره

Now see how they can all be re-expressed using ل . **Read and write:**

المدير للبنك   المدير للبنك   al-mudīr li-l-bank

النمرة للشركة   النمره للشرك   an-numra li-sh-sharika

نمرة التلفون للمكتب*   نمرة التلفون للمكتب
numrat at-tilifōn li-l-maktab

النمرة للشركة الجديدة**   النمره للشركة الجديره
an-numra li-sh-sharika l-jadīda

النمرة الجديدة للشركة**   النمره الجديره للشرك
an-numra l-jadīda li-sh-sharika

* In this example we have a construct combined with a ل expression.
** Using ل here makes it clear what is new: the company or its number.
You will see this use of ل in many advertisements, headlines and notices.

7 Descriptions, Equations and Constructs
We have studied three basic structures. It may be useful to summarise and compare their commonest forms here, to avoid confusion:

	1st Part	2nd Part	Example	
Description	definite	definite	المكتب الكبير	*the big office*
	indefinite	indefinite	مكتب كبير	*a big office*
Equation	definite	indefinite	المكتب كبير.	*The office is big.*
Construct	indefinite in form	definite	مكتب المدير	*the manager's office*
		indefinite	مكتب مدير	*a manager's office*

Exercise 7 Read out and translate these newspaper report headings:

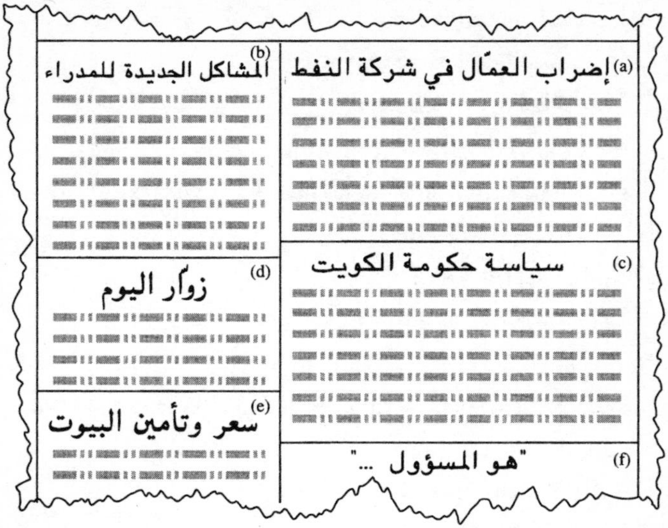

Which expressions are constructs? Definite? Indefinite? Any 'compound' or 'string' constructs (paragraph 4 above)? What are those expressions which are not constructs?

The answers are given immediately below.

Answers to Exercises

Exercise 1 (a) **qism al-ḥisābāt** *Accounts Department*
(b) **madkhal al-wizāra** *Ministry Entrance*
(c) **mudīr al-maktab** *Office Manager*
(d) **qism at-tasjīl** *Registration Department*
(e) **istiqbāl az-zuwwār** *Visitor ('Visitors') Reception*
(f) **maktab al-madfū9āt** *Payments Office*

Exercise 2 (a) **مكتب العقود maktab al-9uqūd** *Contracts Office*
(b) **قسم الهندسة qism al-handasa** *Engineering Department*
(c) **تأمين بيتي ta'mīn baytī** *my house insurance*
(d) **شغل الوزارة shughl al-wizāra** *the ministry's work*

Exercise 3 (a) قسم المرور **qism al-murūr**, right
(b) مكتب الضرائب **maktab aḍ-ḍarā'ib**, left
(c) تسجيل السيارات **tasjīl as-sayyārāt**, left
(d) إصدار الرخص **iṣdār ar-ru<u>kh</u>aṣ**, right

Exercise 4 (a) وزارة العمل **wizārat al-9amal**
(b) وزارة التربية **wizārat at-tarbiya,** وزارة التعليم **wizārat at-ta9līm**
(c) وزترة الدفاع **wizārat ad-difā9**
(d) وزارة الزراعة **wizārat az-zirā9a**
(e) وزارة الصناعة **wizārat aṣ-ṣinā9a**

Exercise 5 (a) دائرة العمل **dā'irat al-9amal**
(b) دائرة التربية **dā'irat at-tarbiya,** دائرة التعليم **dā'irat at-ta9līm**
(c) دائرة الدفاع **dā'irat ad-difā9**
(d) دائرة الزراعة **dā'irat az-zirā9a**
(e) دائرة الصناعة **dā'irat aṣ-ṣinā9a**

Exercise 6 (a) رئيس وزارة **ra'īs wizāra** *head of a ministry*
(b) مدير شركة **mudīr <u>sh</u>arika** *a company manager*
(c) نمرة سيارة **numrat sayyāra** *a car number*
(d) تسجيل عقد **tasjīl 9aqd** *registration of a contract*

Exercise 7 (a) **iḍrāb al-9ummāl fī <u>sh</u>arikat an-nafṭ** *Workers' Strike in ('the') Oil Company*, two definite constructs connected with **fī**
(b) **al-ma<u>sh</u>ākil al-jadīda li-l-mudarā'** *Managers' New Problems*, not a construct but a definite description (Unit 9) and expression with ل
(c) **siyāsat ḥukūmat al-kuwayt** *Kuwait Government Policy*, definite 'string' construct
(d) **zuwwār al-youm** *Today's Visitors*, definite construct
(e) **si9r wa-ta'mīn al-buyūt** *Cost and Insurance of ('the') Houses*, definite compound construct
(f) **huwa l-mas'ūl**, *He is the one responsible*, not a construct but an equation with a definite second part (Unit 10).

Tests

1 Make as many meaningful constructs as possible, using a word from (a) to (e) as first noun and a word from (f) to (k) as second noun. Read each construct aloud and translate it. Is it definite or indefinite?

(a) وزارة (b) مدير (c) مكتب
(d) دائرة (e) مشاكل
(f) الشركة (g) التجارة (h) الجمرك
(j) الخارجية (k) زميل

2 Rewrite the word, filling in the missing letter. Read your answer aloud.

(a) ...دراء (b) تقر..ر (c) ا...تظار
(d) إضـ..ـاب (e) مسـ..ـول

3 Rewrite these constructs as expressions with ل . Read your answer aloud and translate it.

(a) تأمين البيت الجديد (b) سيارة زميلي المصري
(c) مشاكل القسم الإداري (d) في مكتب الجمرك
(e) شركة تأمين

4 Make these expressions plural. Read your answer aloud and translate it:

(a) مشكلة كبيرة (b) زائر أجنبي (c) مدير وموظّف
(d) عامل عربي (e) مأمور مصري

Review

You are now armed with a total vocabulary of just over 300 words, and three very important structures. Together, these should make intelligible much of what you see around you in signs, notices and advertisements.

You now have the knowledge to copy an unknown word or phrase accurately and later ask an Arab about it. Don't be shy about your pronunciation; listen to what you hear around you and try to imitate it, bearing in mind the brief instructions given in this book. Speak up. You learn by doing.

We now move on to the numbers, the time and the date.

13

In this unit you will learn

- numbers,
- the clock and the calendar.

New Words: * **الوقت والنقود al-waqt wa-n-nuqūd** *Time and Money*

1 *Essential Vocabulary*

بعد الظّهر	**ba9d aẓ-ẓuḥr** *afternoon*	شهر أشهر	**shahr ashhur** *month*
تاريخ تواريخ	**tārīkh tawārīkh** *date*	صباح	**ṣabāḥ** *morning*
جنيه	**jinayh** *pound (£)*	صباحًا	**ṣabāḥan** *a.m.*
درهم دراهم	**dirham darāhim** *dirham*	صرّاف	**ṣarrāf** *money changer*
دقيقة دقائق	**daqīqa daqā'iq** *minute*	صرف	**ṣarf** *exchange*
دولار	**dōlār** *dollar*	ظهر	**ẓuḥr** *midday*
دينار دنانير	**dīnār danānīr** *dinar*	مدّة مدد	**mudda mudad** *period*
ساعة	**sā9a** *hour*	*مصرف مصارف	**maṣrif maṣārif** *bank*
سنة سنوات	**sana sanawāt** *year*	يوم أيّام	**youm ayyām** *day*

* In speech, use the popular words for *money*, فلوس **fulūs** (inanimate plural) and *bank*, بنك بنوك, the latter already known to you.

Numbers

2 Look back to Unit 7, paragraph 4, for the explanation of the Arabic numerals.

The officially correct pronunciation of the numbers, and their variable spelling as words, is complicated. Most Arabs (including educated Arabs) have difficulty with it; they prefer to use a greatly simplified colloquial pronunciation, and to avoid writing the figures in words. You are strongly advised to do the same. The colloquial pronunciation varies, but the version given below is understood and accepted by all Arabs. Beside the pronunciation you will find the variable official spellings, for recognition only. For once you are *not* being asked to 'Read and Write':

0 ٠ (صفر) **ṣifr** | **1** ١ (واحد\واحدة) **wāḥid(a)**

2 ٢ (اثنان\اثنتان\اثنين\اثنتين) **ithnayn, thintayn**

3	٣	(ثلاثة\ثلاث)	thalātha	4	٤	(أربعة\أربع)	arba9a
5	٥	(خمسة\خمس)	khamsa	6	٦	(ستّة\ستّ)	sitta
7	٧	(سبعة\سبع)	sab9a	8	٨	(ثمانية\ثمان)	thamāniya
9	٩	(تسعة\تسع)	tis9a	10	١٠	(عشرة\عشر)	9ashra

We need to note:

- **wāḥid** and **ithnayn** are masculine, **wāḥida** and **thintayn** are feminine. In counting without a noun, we use the masculine form.
- Numbers **3** to **10** have only one spoken form. A noun following a number from **3** to **10** is made plural:

٦ عمّال **(sitta)** *six workmen*   ١٠ ريالات **(9ashra)** *ten riyals*

It may be enough for you to know the numbers up to **10**; that suffices for reading out any number. In that case, do Exercise 1 below and stop there. You can, if you wish, skim through paragraphs 3 to 7 below and treat them as reference material.

Exercise 1 In this fragment of the telephone book, find the numbers of (a) Hassan Abu Issa (b) Jamal Abu Issa (c) Hamad Abu Issa

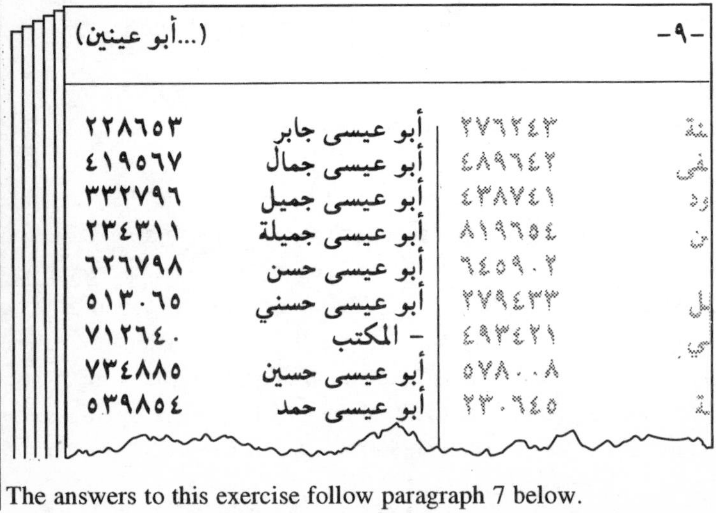

(أبو عينين...)			-٩-
٢٢٨٦٥٣	أبو عيسى جابر	٢٧٦٢٤٣	نة
٤١٩٥٦٧	أبو عيسى جمال	٤٨٩٦٤٢	فى
٣٣٢٧٩٦	أبو عيسى جميل	٤٣٨٧٤١	ود
٢٣٤٣١١	أبو عيسى جميلة	٨١٩٦٥٤	ن
٦٢٦٧٩٨	أبو عيسى حسن	٦٤٥٩٠٢	
٥١٣٠٦٥	أبو عيسى حسني	٢٧٩٤٣٣	يل
٧١٢٦٤٠	- المكتب	٤٩٣٤٢١	ي
٧٣٤٨٨٥	أبو عيسى حسين	٥٧٨٠٠٨	
٥٣٩٨٥٤	أبو عيسى حمد	٢٣٠٦٤٥	ة

The answers to this exercise follow paragraph 7 below.

3 If you wish to go further with the numbers, here are first eleven to twenty, in colloquial pronunciation without the script:

11	**١١**	**iḥd9ashar**	**12**	**١٢**	**ithn9ashar**
13	**١٣**	**thalatt9ashar**	**14**	**١٤**	**arba9t9ashar**
15	**١٥**	**khamst9ashar**	**16**	**٦**	**sitt9ashar**
17	**١٧**	**sab9at9ashar**	**18**	**٨**	**thamant9ashar**
19	**١٩**	**tis9at9ashar**	**20**	**٢٠**	**9ishrīn**

The tens from thirty to ninety:

30	**٣٠**	**thalāthīn**	**40**	**٤٠**	**arba9īn**
50	**٥٠**	**khamsīn**	**60**	**٦٠**	**sittīn**
70	**٧٠**	**sab9īn**	**80**	**٨٠**	**thamānīn, thamāniyīn**
90	**٩٠**	**tis9īn**			

Compounds with the tens are assembled like 'five-and-twenty' with the units first, joined to the tens with و *and*, pronounced colloquially **u-**. Pronounce:

21	**٢١**	**wāḥid u-9ishrīn**	**32**	**٣٢**	**ithnayn u-thalāthīn**

From one hundred upwards, you need to recognise in script only *a hundred*, *a thousand* and *a million*:

100	١٠٠	مئة\مائة	**mīya***
1000	١٠٠٠	ألف	**alf**
1 million	١٠٠٠ ٠٠٠	مليون	**milyūn**

Here are the duals, without the script:

200	٢٠٠	**mitayn**
2000	٢٠٠٠	**alfayn**
2 million	٢٠٠٠ ٠٠٠	**milyūnayn**

Then the other compounds, for which we use the singular of *hundred* but the plurals of *thousand* and *million*:

300-900 ٩٠٠-٣٠٠ **thalāthmīya, arba9mīya, khamsmīya, sittmīya, saba9mīya, thamanmīya, tisa9mīya***

* **mīya** and its multiples become **mīt** before a noun:

١٠٠ موظف **mīt muwaẓẓaf** 100 employees

٥٠٠ سنة <u>kh</u>amsmīt sana 500 years

3000-9000　٩٠٠٠-٣٠٠٠　<u>th</u>alā<u>th</u>a, arba9a (etc.) *t*ālāf (NB)

3-9 million　٩٠٠٠٠٠٠-٣٠٠٠٠٠٠　<u>th</u>alā<u>th</u>a (etc.) malāyīn

Read these higher compound numbers now. Note how we have **u-** *and* between the elements:

٦٤٢　sittmīya u-<u>th</u>nayn u-arba9īn

٣٤٨٩　<u>th</u>alā<u>th</u>a tālāf u-'arba9mīya u-tis9a u-<u>th</u>amānīn

A noun following a number takes different forms depending on the number. Don't be confused by the different forms - you will sometimes see singulars, with or without **tanwīn** (Unit 6, paragraph 3), and sometimes plurals. There is no need to learn the rules; simply read the noun as you see it:

٥ دنانير　<u>kh</u>amsa danānīr *five dinars*

١٥ ديناراً　<u>kh</u>amst9a<u>sh</u>ar dīnāran *fifteen dinars*

١٥٠ دينار　mīya u-<u>kh</u>amsīn dīnār *150 dinars*

Exercise 2 Translate:

(a) ٥٠٠ ريال　(b) ٣٦٥ يومًا　(c) ٤٦ دولارًا (d) ٢٤ ساعة (e) دينارين

Exercise 3 Write these numbers in Arabic figures:

(a) *450*　　(b) *2028*　　(c) *779 4391*　　(d) *404 836*　　(e) *99-2440*

The answers to these exercises follow paragraph 7 below.

4　Ordinal numbers

The ordinal numbers ('first, second, third') are not difficult, and the official pronunciation is used. We need learn only 'first' to 'twelfth'. The ordinal numbers are almost always definite. *Read and write:*

the 1st　الأوّل الأوَّلى　m. الأوّل al-'awwal, f. الأولى al-'ūla

the 2nd　الثاني الثانيه　m. الثّاني a<u>th</u>-<u>th</u>ānī, f. الثّانية a<u>th</u>-<u>th</u>ániya

the 3rd　الثالث الثالثه　m. الثّالث a<u>th</u>-<u>th</u>āli<u>th</u>, f. الثّالثة a<u>th</u>-<u>th</u>āli<u>th</u>a

the 4th	الرابع	الرّابع	**ar-rābi9**
the 5th	الخامس	الخامس	**al-khāmis**
the 6th	السادس	السّادس	**as-sādis**
the 7th	السابع	السّابع	**as-sābi9**
the 8th	الثامن	الثامن	**ath-thāmin**
the 9th	التاسع	التّاسع	**at-tāsi9**
the 10th	العاشر	العاشر	**al-9āshir**
the 11th	الحادي عشر	الحادي عشر	**al-ḥādī 9ashar**
the 12th	الثاني عشر	الثّاني عشر	**ath-thānī 9ashar**

Note the stress in the f. form thániya (not ***thānīya***). The ordinals from *third* upwards make their feminine form in the usual way.

You will often find ordinal numbers *first* to *tenth* used in construct, instead of as an adjective. In the construct, both parts are indefinite but, strangely, the meaning is definite; and the m. form is always used, even with a f. noun. ***Read and write:***

للمرّة الثّالثة للمرّة الثالثة **li-l-marra th-thālitha** } *for the third time*

لثالث مرّة لثالث مرّة **li-thālith marra**

We have to write Arabic ordinals as words; there is no way of writing them with figures.

5 Fractions and percentage

We need only *half*, *third* and *quarter* from the fractions. ***Read and write:***

نصف أنصاف نصف انصاف **niṣf anṣāf** *half*

ثلث أثلاث ثلث اثلاث **thulth athlāth** *third*

ربع أرباع ربع ارباع **rub9 arbā9** *quarter*

ثلثين ثلثين **thulthayn** *two-thirds*

٥٠٪ ٥٠٪ **khamsīn bi-l-mīya** *50%*

6 Clock

One o'clock is الساعة الواحدة **as-sā9a l-wāḥida**. Time on the hour above *one* is written as e.g. *the ninth hour*, in definite form. *At* is في .
Read and write:

الساعة الرابعة في الساعة الرابعة في **fi-s-sā9a r-rābi9a**
at four o'clock

الساعة الثانية الساعة الثانية **as-sā9a th-thāniya**
two o'clock

Time in the first half-hour is written as follows. ***Read and write:***

الساعة الثالثة وخمس دقائق الساعة الثالثة وخمس دقائق
(wa-khamsa daqā'iq) *five past three*

الساعة السابعة والربع الساعة السابعة والربع
(wa-r-rub9) *a quarter past seven*

الساعة التاسعة والثلث الساعة التاسعة والثلث
(wa-th-thulth) *twenty past nine*

الساعة الثامنة والنصف الساعة الثامنة والنصف
(wa-n-niṣf) *half-past eight*

Time in the second half-hour is written in the same way, but with إلّا **illa** *'except for, minus'* and the next hour. ***Read and write:***

الساعة الرابعة إلّا عشر دقائق الساعة الرابعة إلّا عشر دقائق
(illa 9ashra daqā'iq) *ten to four*

الساعة الخامسة إلّا الربع الساعة الخامسة إلّا الربع
(illa r-rub9) *a quarter to five*

الساعة السادسة إلّا الثلث الساعة السادسة إلّا الثلث
(illa th-thulth) *twenty to six*

Time written in figures is shown as follows. The style of comma may vary, and may even be replaced by the letter ر in typescript. Write:

٧,٣٠ ٧ر٣٠ *7.30* ٤,١٥ ٤,١٥ *4.15* ١٠،٢٥ ١٠،٢٥ *10.25*

7 Calendar

Read and write the days of the week:

السبت	السّبت	**as-sabt** *Saturday*
الأحد	الأحد	**al-'aḥad** *Sunday*
الاثنين	الاثنين	**al-ithnayn** *Monday*
الثلاثاء	الثلاثاء	**ath-thalātha*** *Tuesday*
الأربعاء	الأربعاء	**al-'arba9a*** *Wednesday*
الخميس	الخميس	**al-khamīs** *Thursday*
الجمعة	الجمعة	**al-jum9a** *Friday*

* colloquial pronunciation, almost universal.

The names of the days may be preceded by يوم **youm** *day*, in construct. *On* with a day is في:

في يوم السبت في يوم السبت **fī youm as-sabt** *on Saturday*

Here are the names of the months. There are two sets of names, one used in African, the other in Asian Arab countries:

	Africa		*Asia*	
January	يناير	**yanāyir**	كانون الثاني	**kānūn ath-thānī**
February	فبراير	**fibrāyir**	شباط	**shubāṭ**
March	مارس	**māris**	آذار	**ādhār**
April	أبريل	**abrīl**	نيسان	**nīsān**
May	مايو	**māyū**	أيار	**ayār**
June	يونيو	**yūniyū**	حزيران	**ḥazīrān**
July	يوليو	**yūliyū**	تمّوز	**tammūz**
August	أغسطس	**aghusṭus**	آب	**āb**
September	سبتمبر	**sibtambir**	أيلول	**aylūl**

October	أكتوبر	oktōbir	تشرين الأوّل	ti<u>sh</u>rīn al-awwal
November	نوفمبر	nūfimbir	تشرين الثّاني	ti<u>sh</u>rīn a<u>th</u>-<u>th</u>ānī
December	دسمبر	disambir	كانون الأوّل	kānūn al-awwal

The Islamic calendar is also in use in some countries. The Islamic year is 354 or 355 days long. The year-count starts from the day of the flight of the prophet Muḥammad from Mecca to Medina, in 622 AD. Here are the names of the twelve months:

صفر	ṣafar	٢	محرّم	muharram	١
ربيع الثاني	rabī9 a<u>th</u>-<u>th</u>ānī	٤	ربيع الأوّل	rabī9 al-awwal	٣
جمادى الآخرة	jumāda l-'ā<u>kh</u>ira	٦	جمادى الأولى	jumāda l-'ūla	٥
شعبان	<u>sh</u>a9bān	٨	رجب	rajab	٧
شوّال	<u>sh</u>awwāl	١٠	رمضان	ramaḍān	٩
ذو الحجّة	<u>dh</u>u l-ḥijja	١٢	ذو القعدة	<u>dh</u>u l-qa9da	١١

Dates are expressed with أوّل for the first of the month, and the ordinal numbers thereafter. Here are two typical dates, with the (colloquial) pronunciation:

م١٩٨٤\٧\٢٠   9i<u>sh</u>rīn yūliyū/tammūz sanat alf u-tisa9mīya u-'arba9a u-<u>th</u>amānīn al-mīlādīya 20/7/1984 AD.

هـ١٤١٩\٧\١   awwal rajab sanat alf u-'arba9mīya u-tis9at9a<u>sh</u>ar al-hijrīya 25/7/1419 AH.

In these dates, م is ميلادية 'AD'; هـ is هجرية 'AH' which is Anno Hegiræ, the Year of the Flight.

Exercise 4 Read aloud these dates, in the Western calendar, with both Arabic forms for each month:

٢٠٠١\٨\١ (c)   ١٩٩٩\٤\٢٤ (b)   ٢٠٠٢\١٢\١٢ (a)

The answers to this exercise are on the next page.

Answers to Exercises

Exercise 1 (a) 626798 (line 5) (b) 419567 (line 2) (c) 539854 (line 9)

Exercise 2 (a) 500 riyals (b) 365 days (c) 46 dollars (d) 24 hours (e) 2 dinars

Exercise 3 (a) ٤٥٠ (b) ٢٠٢٨ (c) ٧٧٩ ٤٣٩١ (d) ٤٠٤ ٨٣٦ (e) ٩٩-٢٤٤٠

Exercise 4 (a) **ithn9ashar disambir/kānūn al-'awwal sanat alfayn u-thnayn**
(b) **arba9a u-ishrīn abrīl/nīsān sanat alf u-tisa9mīya u-tis9a u-tis9īn**
(c) **awwal aghusṭus/āb sanat alfayn u-wāḥid**

Tests

1 Read aloud and translate. (The spelling of some numbers written as words will be unfamiliar. Pronounce as shown in this unit, irrespective of the spelling.):

(a) ستّة أسابيع (b) خمسمئة ريال (c) في الساعة الثامنة
(d) ١٥٪ (e) عشرين جنيه مصري
(f) في سنة ١٩٩٩ (g) جنيهين (h) بعد الساعة ٧،٣٠
(j) صباحًا (k) ثلاثة آلاف ليرة

2 Read out and translate the time:

(a) ٨,١٥ (b) الساعة الرابعة إلاّ الثلث (c) ١٢,٢٥

Review

For the cardinal numbers, you should use the unofficial spoken form, which is always acceptable, when reading aloud. (In fact, quoting the numbers in official form is often regarded as somewhat precious.)

For writing the cardinal numbers, use the figures.

In the next unit we look briefly at the geography of the Arab world.

14

In this unit you will learn

- important vocabulary for the Arab world.

New Words: العالم العربي al-9ālam al-9arabī *The Arab World*

1 It is not possible to divide this vocabulary into essential and non-essential for you; only you can do that, depending on your situation and your needs.

Vocabulary - Arab World

أبو ظبي **abū ẓabī** *Abu Dhabi*
الأردن **al-’urdun** *Jordan*
الإسكندرية **al-’iskandarīya** *Alexandria*
البحرين **al-baḥrayn** *Bahrain*
بغداد **baghdād** *Baghdad*
بيروت **bayrūt** *Beirut*
تونس **tūnis** *Tunis(ia)*
الجزائر **al-jazā’ir** *Algeria, Algiers*
الخرطوم **al-khartūm** *Khartoum*
دبي **dubayy** *Dubai*
دمشق **dimashq** *Damascus*
الدّوحة **ad-douḥa** *Doha*
الرباط **ar-ribāṭ** *Rabat*
الرّياض **ar-riyāḍ** *Riyadh*
السّعودي **as-sa9ūdīya** *Saudi Arabia*
السودان **as-sūdān** *Sudan*
طرابلس **ṭarābulus** *Tripoli*
عمان **9umān** *Oman*
عمّان **9ammān** *Amman*
فلسطين **filasṭīn** *Palestine*
القدس **al-quds** *Jerusalem*
قطر **qaṭar** *Qatar*
الكويت **al-kuwayt** *Kuwait*
مسقط **masqaṭ** *Muscat*
المغرب **al-maghrib** *Morocco*
موريتانية **mūrītāniya** *Mauritania*
اليمن **al-yaman** *Yemen*
الأراضي المحتلّة **al-’arāḍī l-muḥtalla** *the occupied territories*
الإمارات (العربية المتّحدة) **al-’imārāt (al-9arabīya l-muttaḥida)** *(United Arab) Emirates*
البحر الأبيض المتوسّط **al-baḥr al-’abyaḍ al-mutawassiṭ** *Mediterranean Sea*
البحر الأحمر **al-baḥr al-’aḥmar** *the Red Sea*
الدّار البيضاء **ad-dār al-bayḍā’** *Casablanca*
الخليج (العربي) **al-khalīj (al-9arabī)** *the (Arabian) Gulf*

Exercise 1 Give the Arabic names of countries (a) to (e) and cities (f) to (k) marked on the map of the Arab world following Exercise 2 below.

Exercise 2 Situate the following places on the map:

(a) البحر الأبيض المتوسّط (b) الخليج (c) البحر الأحمر (d) ايران
(e) إيطاليا

بلدان ومدن عربية

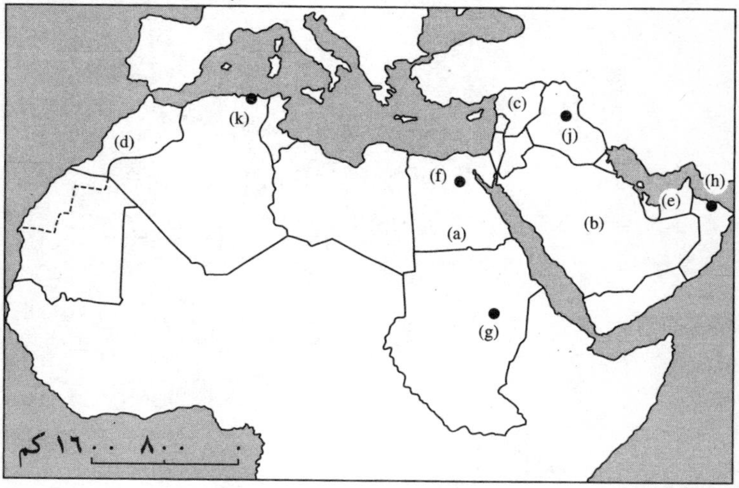

The answers are given on the next page.

Answers to Exercises

Exercise 1 (a) مصر (b) العربية السعودية (c) سوريا (d) المغرب (e) الإمارات العربية المتّحدة (f) القاهرة (g) الخرطوم (h) مسقط (j) بغداد (k) الجزائر

Exercise 2 This map shows the answers, and also all the Arab countries:

العالم العربي وإيطاليا وإيران

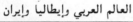

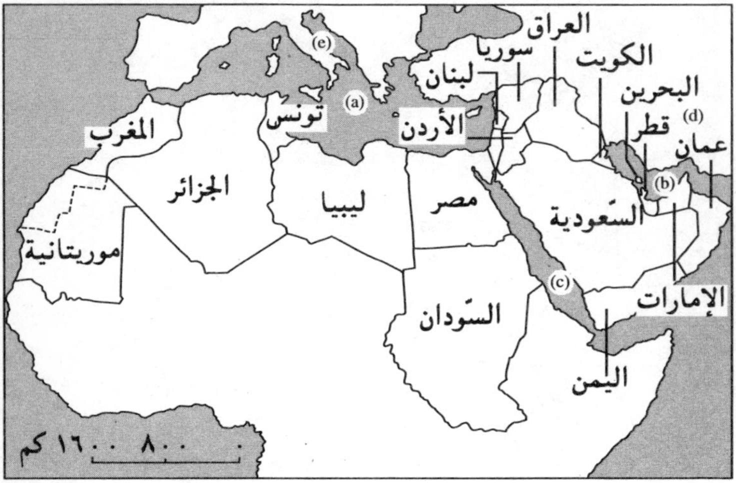

Tests

1 Make masculine singular relatives, and translate your answer:

(a) اليمن (b) عمان (c) قطر
(d) المغرب (e) موريتانية

2 Complete the calculation in Arabic figures, and read your answer aloud:

(a) ٢٤ × ٤ = *(b) ١٨٠ : ٣ =
(c) ١٥٥ − ٨٥ = (d) ٤ + ٣ + ٢ =
(e) £٤٠ − ٥٪ = * (: is ÷)

Review

مبروك! Congratulations. I hope some of the mystery is now unlocked for you. Keep practising, with every sign, notice, number, advertisement etc. that you set your eyes on. And *write things down.*

Don't forget what is said in the Introduction about roots. You can often untangle an unknown word by applying two tests:

- Do *three consonants* in the word also occur, in the same order, in a word which you know? If so, you have a basic meaning, and the word is probably closely associated with it.
- Is the *pattern* of the word familiar? Is it a participle, a verbal noun, an adjective? Is it a relative? An irregular plural?
  If that works, then you have scored in a further two areas:
  - you know what sort of word it is,
  - you can add the short vowels and pronounce the word.

If you get that far, you can make an informed guess at the meaning of the new word; and, knowing its function, you can use the word correctly in a structure.

Treat this book also as a reference manual. That is the main purpose of the two vocabularies and the index at the back. Don't try to learn vocabulary by heart, but rather let it come with practice.

We now move on to your final Reading Test.

15

Test Your Reading

This unit tests how well you can read now. You get no help: we are under field conditions. You can do it. Use the vocabulary only in emergency. The answers are in the key at the back of the book.

Signs

Test 1

Where are we going, and how far is it?

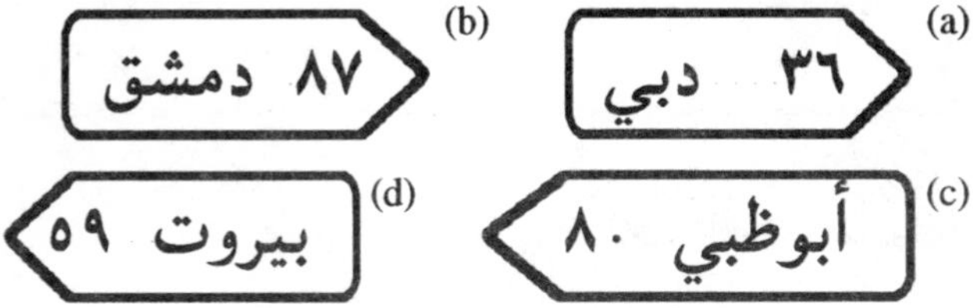

Test 2

What is left, what is right, and what is straight on?

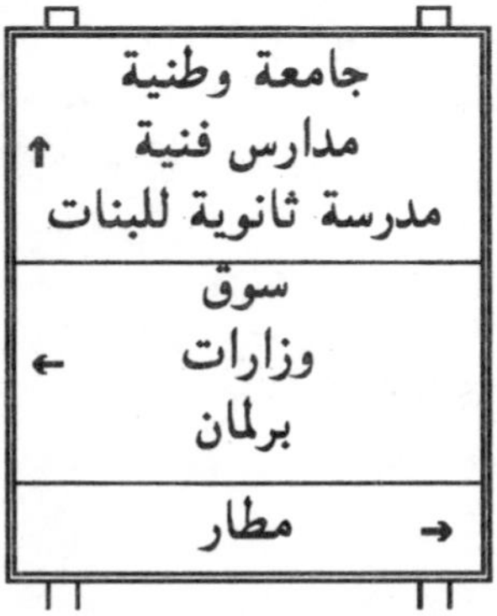

Test 3

What must you do, what can't you do, and what are you requested to do?

(a) قف وراء الخطّ

(b) ممنوع التدخين

(c) ممنوع الدخول

(d) الرجاء الانتظار هنا

Test 4

What part of town are we in?

(a) شارع عبد الناصر

(b) ميدان الاستقلال

(c) حيّ رقم ٦

(d) شارع القصر الجديد

Headlines

Test 5

Read the headlines aloud and translate them:

(a) شركات بريطانية في المعرض الزراعي

(b) الكل ضد تقسيم العراق..

(c) العلاقات الاسرائيلية - الأميركية

Small print

Test 6

Look at these items and answer the questions.

(a)

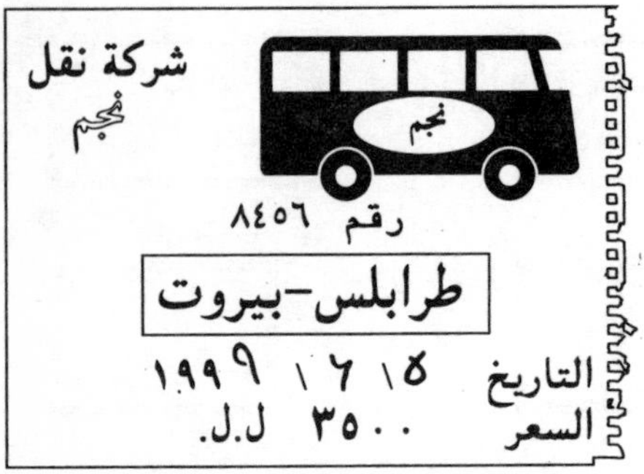

This ticket was issued by a company called Najm. What sort of ticket is it? What can you do with it? What did it cost? Make a guess at 'ل.ل'. When was this ticket issued, and what is its serial number?

(b)

Who issued this banknote? What are its value and its serial number? Read aloud and translate the very small text at the top left-hand side which says:

بيروت في ٢٢ تشرين الثاني سنة ١٩٩٠

Handwriting

Test 7

Match the handwritten forms (a) to (e) with the typewritten forms (f) to (k). Read them aloud:

(a) تفتيش السيارات

(b) ممنوع من مساعدتك

(c) في السوق

(d) السيد ابو حنيفة

(e) من بيروت الى عمّان

(f)

(g)

(h)

(j)

(k)

Test 8

Read this handwritten note aloud and translate it:

السيد "براون": السائق ابوبكر حاضر في الساعة
السابعة والنصف صباحاً لزيارة الجيزة.

Using a directory

Test 9

Put these directory entries into alphabetical order:

وزارة المالية، أبوبكر، بلدية، مجلس الثقافة، شلّ لبنان، مدرسة ثانوية، سفارة تونس، غرفة التجارة، نجم، المكتبة الحديثة.

Test 10

Under what Arabic word would you first look for the following in a telephone book?

(a) Nimr Bus Company (b) Kuwaiti Embassy (c) Munir Rais & Sons (d) Habib's Insurance (e) El-Nur Moroccan Restaurant

If that didn't work, under what word would you make your second attempt? And any further attempts?

KEY to TESTS

Unit 1

1 (b) بيتين (c) ابني (d) اثاثي (e) نبات

2 (b) baytáyn (c) íbnī (d) athā́thī (e) nabā́t

3 (b) i<u>th</u>náyn (c) yābā́nī (d) áyna (e) íbnī

4 (b) بنتين (c) بناياتي (d) بابين (e)اين (f) اثاثي

5 (b) bāb; middle alif (c) āb; alif madda (d) nabā́t; middle alif
   (e) i<u>th</u>náyn; alif at the beginning shows a short vowel (here, i)

Unit 2

1 (b)التمويل (c) اوّل (d) الماني (e) ممنون

2 (b) at-tamwī́l (c) áwwal (d) almā́nī (e) mamnū́n

3 (b) áwwal (c) a<u>th</u>-<u>th</u>ā́li<u>th</u> (d) mamnū́n (e) an-naml

4 (b) ممثّلين (c)التمويل (d) النّيلين (e) او (f) اليابني

5   الماني، ياباني، لبناني، ليبي   nationalities
  الثالث، اوّل، اثنين، ثلاث   numbers
  يونيو، يوليو، آب، مايو   months
  البيوت، البنايات   buildings

Unit 3

1 (b)الاسم (c)الممثّل (d) أنباء (e) ثنائي

2 (b) al-ism (c) al-mumá<u>ththi</u>l (d) anbā́' (e) <u>th</u>unā́ʼī

3 (b) al-lubnānī́ya (c) al-'almānī́ya (d) bi-l-'áwwal
   (e) bi-<u>th</u>-<u>th</u>ā́li<u>th</u>a

4 (b) ياباني (c) اللبناني (d) مسؤول (e) للثالث

5 (b) yābā́nī (c) al-lubnā́nī (d) mas'ū́l (e) li-<u>th</u>-<u>th</u>ā́li<u>th</u>

6 (b) اهتمام (c)الملابس (d) البيوت (e) ثانوي

Unit 4

1 (a) مصرية (b) اهتمام (c) تمام (d) ضروري (e) الماني

2 (a) **miṣrī́ya** (b) **ihtimā́m** (c) **tamā́m** (d) **ḍarū́rī** (e) **almā́nī**

3 (a) **al-'īrānī́ya** (b) **marī́ḍ** (c) **li-s-sūrī́ya** (d) **ibtidā́'ī** (e) **bi-l-'almā́niya**

4 (a) أساس *basis,* أساسي *basic* (b) دراسة *study,* دراسي *academic*
(c) إدارة *administration,* إداري *administrative*
(d) ليبيا *Libya,* لليبية *for the Libyan (woman)*
(e) إسرائيل *Israel,* الإسرائيلية *the Israeli (woman)*

5 (a) **asā́s** (b) **dirā́sa** (c) **idā́ra** (d) **lī́biya** (e) **isrā'ī́l**

6 (a) المصرية (b) إدارة (c) مدير (d) الشّيء (e) مريضة

Unit 5

1 (a) **ash-shay'** *the thing* (b) **mas'ūla** *responsible*
(c) **as-si9r** *the price* (d) **madkhal** *entrance*
(e) **al-intikhāb** *the election*

2 (a) السّنة (b) الشّهر (c) الأسبوع (d) اليوم

3 (a) صناعي *industrial* (b) ابتدائي *initial, primary*
(c) أسبوعي *weekly* (d) إيطالي *Italian* (e) بريطاني *British*

4 (a) التّأسيس (b) النّهائي (c) مسؤولة (d) المخرج (e) الدّخول

Unit 6

1 (a) **ṣinā9a** *industry* (b) **maṭār** *airport* (c) **mas'ūl** *responsible*
(d) **wizāra** *ministry* (e) **idāra** *administration* (f) **akhbār** *news*
(g) **iḥtijāj** *objection* (h) **sharika** *company* (j) **ow** *or* (k) **sūq** *market*
(m) **mathalan** *for example* (n) **mustashfa** *hospital*

2 (a) معلّم **mu9allim** (b) مكتب **maktab** (c) فوراً **fouran**
(d) تأسيس **ta'sīs** (e) ابتدائي **ibtidā'ī**

3 (a) *Kodak* (b) *IBM* (c) *Mobil* (d) *Michelin* (e) *Peugeot*

Unit 7

1 (a) **al-9irāq** *Iraq* (b) **al-qāhira** *Cairo* (c) **sharika** *company* (d) **mumkin** *possible* (e) **ziyāra** *visit* (f) **idārī** *administrative* (g) **mumaththilīn** *representatives* (h) **as-sūrīyīn** *the Syrians* (j) **maḥkama** *law-court* (k) **ajnabī** *foreign* (m) **madāris** *schools* (n) **al-intikhābāt** *the elections*

2 مدارس، مشاكل، مطاعم، عواصم، مبالغ، محاكم
أسابيع، أساليب
بيوت، خطوط، ظروف، بنوك
أخبار، أرقام، أموال، أفكار
مدراء، وزراء، وكلاء

3 (a) سوريين (b) إيرانيين (c) مصريين (d) عراقيين (e) كويتيين

4 (a) البنايات (b) السّفارات (c) مستشفيات (d) كمبوترات
(e) إوتيلات (f) معلّمات (g) المطارات (h) منظّمات
(j) شركات (k) إمكانيات (m) الزّيارات (n) انتخابات

Unit 8

1 (a) **taqdīm** verbal noun (b) **rākib** active participle (c) **murāsil** active participle (d) **indhār** verbal noun (e) **musta9lim** active participle (f) **shāmil** active participle (g) **iftitāḥ** verbal noun (h) **sāmi9** active participle (j) **mudarris** active participle (k) **istithmār** verbal noun

2 (a) مناسبة (b) انتخابي (c) مقرّرين (d) عمّال (e) تنظيم

3 (a) مفتّش **mufattish** *inspector,* تفتيش **taftīsh** *inspection*
(b) مشترك **mushtarik** *joint, common,* اشتراك **ishtirāk** *participation*
(c) مرسل **mursil** *sender,* إرسال **irsāl** *despatch*
(d) مساعد **musā9id** *assistant,* مساعدة **musā9ada** *help*
(e) مستقبل **mustaqbil** *receiver,* استقبال **istiqbāl** *reception*

4 (a) **al-istiqbāl** (b) **madrasa li-l-banāt** (c) **miṣr wa-l-9irāq** (d) **īrān** (e) **al-qāhira**

Unit 9

1 (a) **ṣiḥāfatna l-'usbū9īya** *our weekly press*
(b) **iḥtijājāthum aṭ-ṭawīla** *their long objections*
(c) **az-zumala' al-fannīyīn** *the technical colleagues*
(d) **ṣuḥuf 9arabīya** *Arab(ic) newspapers*
(e) **bank ajnabī** *a foreign bank*

2 (a) مدرسة ابتدائية (b) المطار الوطني (c) تقاريره اليومية
(d) لزوّارنا الأجانب (e) انتخابات عامّة

3 (a) رسالات طويلة (b) التقارير الفنّية (c) ممثّلين أجانب
(d) الطائرات الأميركية (e) خطوط جوّية

Unit 10

1 (a) **waẓīfatu ṣa9ba.** *His job is difficult.*
(b) **al-mu'tamar at-tijārī hāmm.**
The trade conference is important.
(c) **al-wuzarā' moujūdūn.** *The ministers are present.*
(d) **aṣ-ṣūra jamīla.** *The picture/photograph is beautiful.*
(e) **aṣ-ṣūra l-jamīla** *the beautiful picture/photograph*

2 (a) الموظّفون مسرورون. **al-muwaẓẓafūn masrūrūn**
The employees are pleased.
(b) مطارنا الدولي هامّ. **maṭārna d-duwalī hāmm.**
Our international airport is important.
(c) هو تاجر دولي. **huwa tājir duwalī.**
He is an international trader.
(d) النصّ واضح ومقبول. **an-naṣṣ wāḍiḥ wa-maqbūl.**
The text is clear and acceptable.
(e) المأمور مشغول. **al-ma'mūr ma<u>shgh</u>ūl.** *The official is busy.*

3 (a) وظيفة **waẓīfa** *job* (b) موظّف **muwaẓẓaf** *employee*
(c) مندوب **mandūb** *delegate* (d) غائب **<u>gh</u>ā'ib** *absent*
(e) الخبراء **al-<u>kh</u>ubarā'** *the experts*

Unit 11

1 (a) **mamnū9 al-intiẓār** *WAITING PROHIBITED*

(b) **fi l-balad** *in (the) town*

(c) **fi l-bilād** *in the towns/in the country*

(d) **ashghāl 9ala ṭ-ṭarīq** *road works ('works on the road')*

(e) **al-murūr ila l-yamīn** *turning right*

2 (a) سيّارات جديدة (b) أشغال هامّة (c) الشّرطة المحلّية

(d) مستشفيات كبيرة (e) مشاكل فنّية

3 (a) **al-ma'mūr al-mas'ūl** *the responsible official*; Description

(b) **al-ma'mūrūn hum al-mas'ūlūn** *The officials are those responsible ('the responsible ones').* Equation

(c) **al-bilād jamīl** *The country is beautiful.* Equation

(d) **zamīlī fi l-mustashfa** *My colleague is in hospital.* Equation

(e) **zamīlī l-marīḍ** *my sick colleague;* Description

Unit 12

1 (a) + (g) وزارة التجارة **wizārat at-tijāra**
Ministry of Trade, definite

(a) + (j) وزارة الخارجية **wizārat al-khārijīya**
Ministry of Foreign Affairs, definite

(b) + (f) مدير الشركة **mudīr ash-sharika**
The company director, definite

(b) + (g) مدير التجارة **mudīr at-tijāra** *Director of Trade,* definite

(b) + (h) مدير الجمرك **mudīr al-jumruk**
Director of Customs, definite

(b) + (j) مدير الخرجية **mudīr al-khārijīya**
Director of Foreign Affairs, definite

(c) + (f) مكتب الشركة **maktab ash-sharika**
the company office, definite

(c) + (g) مكتب التجارة **maktab at-tijāra** *Trade Office,* definite

(c) + (h) مكتب الجمرك **maktab al-jumruk**
Customs Office, definite

(c) + (j) مكتب الخارجية **maktab al-khārijīya**
Office of Foreign Affairs, definite

(c) + (k) مكتب زميل **maktab zamīl**
a colleague's office, indefinite

(d) + (g) دائرة التجارة **dā'irat at-tijāra**
Directorate of Trade, definite

(d) + (h) دائرة الجمرك **dā'irat al-jumruk**
Customs Directorate, definite

(d) + (j) دائرة الخارجية **dā'irat al-khārijīya**
Directorate of Foreign Affairs, definite

(e) + (f) مشاكل الشركة **mashākil ash-sharika**
the company's problems, definite

(e) + (g) مشاكل التجارة **mashākil at-tijāra**
the problems of trade, definite

(e) + (h) مشاكل الجمرك **mashākil al-jumruk**
(the) Customs problems, definite

(e) + (j) مشاكل الخارجية **mashākil al-khārijīya**
(the) Foreign Affairs problems, definite

(e) + (k) مشاكل زميل **mashākil zamīl**
a colleague's problems, indefinite

2 (a) مدراء **mudarā'** (b) تقرير **taqrīr** (c) انتظار **intiẓār**
(d) إضراب **iḍrāb** (e) مسؤول **mas'ūl**

3 (a) التأمين للبيت الجديد **at-ta'mīn li-l-bayt al-jadīd**
the insurance of the new house

(b) السيارة لزميلي المصري **as-sayyāra li-zamīlī l-miṣrī**
my Egyptian colleague's car

(c) المشاكل للقسم الإداري **al-mashākil li-l-qism al-'idārī**
Administration Department's problems

(d) في المكتب للجمرك **fi l-maktab li-l-jumruk**
in the Customs Office

(e) شركة للتأمين **sharika li-t-ta'mīn** *an insurance company*

4 (a) مشاكل كبيرة mashākil kabīra *big problems*

(b) زوّار أجانب zuwwār ajānib *foreign visitors*

(c) مدراء وموظفين\...ون mudarā' wa-muwaẓẓafīn/muwaẓẓafūn *directors and employees*

(d) عمّال عرب 9ummāl 9arab *Arab workers*

(e) مأمورين مصريين\مأمورون مصريون ma'mūrīn miṣrīyīn/ ma'mūrūn miṣrīyūn *Egyptian officials*

Unit 13

1 (a) sitt(a) asābī9 *six weeks*

(b) <u>kh</u>amsmīt riyāl *five hundred riyals*

(c) fi s-sā9a <u>th</u>-<u>th</u>āmina *at eight o'clock*

(d) <u>kh</u>amst9a<u>sh</u>ar bi-l-mīya *fifteen per cent*

(e) 9i<u>sh</u>rīn jinayh miṣrī *twenty Egyptian pounds*

(f) fī sanat alf u-tisa9mīya u-tis9a u-tis9īn *in 1999*

(g) jinayhayn *two pounds*

(h) ba9d as-sā9a s-sābi9a wa n-niṣf *after seven-thirty*

(j) ṣabāḥan *a.m./in the morning*

(k) <u>th</u>alā<u>th</u>a tālāf līra *three thousand lira*

2 (a) as-sā9a <u>th</u>-<u>th</u>āmina wa-r-rub9 *a quarter past eight*

(b) as-sā9a r-rābi9a illa <u>th</u>-<u>th</u>ul<u>th</u> *twenty to four*

(c) as-sā9a <u>th</u>-<u>th</u>āniya 9a<u>sh</u>ara wa-<u>kh</u>amsa u-9i<u>sh</u>rīn *twenty-five past twelve*

Unit 14

1 (a) اليمني *(the) Yemeni* (b) عماني *Omani* (c) قطري *Qatari*

(d) المغربي *(the) Moroccan* (e) موريتاني *Mauritanian*

2 (a) ٩٦ = ٤ × ٢٤ sitta u-tis9īn

(b) ٦٠ = ٣ : ١٨٠ sittīn

(c) ٧٠ = ٨٥ − ١٥٥ sab9īn

(d) ٩ = ٢ + ٣ + ٤ tis9a

(e) £٣٨ = ٪٥ − £٤٠ <u>th</u>amāniya u-<u>th</u>alā<u>th</u>īn jinayh

Unit 15

1 (a) *Dubai 36* (b) *Damascus 87* (c) *Abu Dhabi 80* (d) *Beirut 59*

2 Left: *Market, Ministries, Parliament* Right: *Airport*
Straight on: *National University, Technical Schools, Girls' Secondary School*

3 (a) *Stop behind the Line* (b) *No Smoking* (c) *No Entry*
(d) *Please Wait Here*

4 (a) *Abdel Nasser* **(9abd an-nāsir)** *Street* (b) *Independence Square*
(c) *District no. 6* (d) *New Palace Street*

5 (a) **sharikāt barīṭānīya fi l-ma9riḍ az-zirā9ī** *British Companies in Agricultural Exhibition*
(b) **al-kull ḍidd taqsīm al-9irāq** *All are against the partition of Iraq*
(c) **al-9alāqāt al-'isrā'īlīya-al-'amayrkīya** *Israeli-American Relations*

6 (a) A bus ticket from Tripoli (Lebanon) to Beirut. The fare is 3500 Lebanese lira (ل.ل), the date 5/6/1999 and the serial number 8456.
(b) Note issued by the Bank of Lebanon, value 1000 lira, serial number 9205319 $\frac{T3}{7}$. The text reads: **bayrūt fī thnayn u-9ishrīn tishrīn ath-thānī sanat alf u-tisa9mīya u-tis9īn.** *Beirut, 22 November* 1990.

7 (a) and (j) **taftīsh as-sayyārāt**
(b) and (k) **mamnūn min musā9adatak**
(c) and (g) **fi s-sūq**
(d) and (f) **as-sayyid abū ḥasanayn**
(e) and (h) **min bayrūt ila 9ammān**

8 **as-sayyid Brown: as-sāi'q abū bakr ḥāḍir fi s-sā9a s-sābi9a wa-n-niṣf ṣabāḥan li-ziyārat al-gīza.** *Mr Brown: Driver Abu Bakr ready at 7.30 a.m. for the visit to ('of') Giza.*

9 أبو بكر، بلدية، سفارة تونس، شلّ لبنان، غرفة التجارة، مجلس الثقافة، مدرسة ثانوية، المكتبة الحديثة، نجم، وزارة المالية

10 Search in the order shown:
(a) نمر، شركة، أوتوبيس، باص، نقل (b) سفارة، كويت
(c) رئيس، منير، شركة (d) تأمين، حبيب، شركة (e) مطعم، نور

VOCABULARIES

In both these vocabularies:

- Entries are referred by number to the page with the first and other important appearances of the Arabic word.
- Arabic irregular plurals are listed with the singular. Where no plural is shown, it is regular.
- The command form of the verb (pages 94 and 95) is shown with '!' after the English, for clarity.

Arabic-English Vocabulary

For this vocabulary, you can find the alphabetical order of the Arabic letters and non-alphabetical signs on pages 52 and 53. Further, in this vocabulary:

- Arabic irregular plurals are also listed separately with a reference (marked '→') to the singular.
- Words used only or mainly with the article الـ.. are listed with the article, but in the alphabetical position of the word itself.

ا\أ\إ\آ

أب آباء **ab ābā'** *father* 7

آب **āb** *August* 7, 115

آباء → أب

ابتداء **ibtidā'** *beginning* 34

ابتدائي **ibtidā'ī** *initial, primary* 37

أبريل **abrīl** *April* 115

إبل **ibil** *camels* 14

ابن **ibn abnā'** *son* 8

ابناء → ابن

أبو ظبي **abū ẓabī** *Abu Dhabi* 118

أبواب → باب

أبيض → بحر

أثاث **a<u>th</u>ā<u>th</u>** *furniture* 7

أثلاث → ثلث

اثنين **i<u>th</u>nayn** *two* 10, 109; الاثنين **al-i<u>th</u>nayn** *Monday* 115

أجانب → أجنبي

اجتماع **ijtimā9** *meeting* 44, 71

أجر أجور **ajr ujūr** *wage* 84

أجنبي أجانب **ajnabī ajānib** *foreign* 41, 73

أجور → أجر

احتجاج **iḥtijāj** *objection* 41

الأحد **al-'aḥad** *Sunday* 115

أحمر → بحر

أخبار → خبر

أخطار → خطر

أخطبة → خطاب

إدارة **idāra** *administration* 34, 70

آذار **ā<u>dh</u>ār** *March* 115

الأراضي المحتلّة **al-'arāḍī l-muḥtalla** *the occupied territories* 118

أرباع → ربع

الأربعاء **al-'arba9a** *Wednesday* 115

أربعة **arba9a** *four* 110

إرسال **irsāl** *despatch* 70

الأردن **al-'urdun** *Jordan* 118

أرقام → رقم

اركب **irkab** *get on!* 94

أسابيع → أسبوع

أساتذة → أستاذ

أساس أسس **asās usus** *basis* 29

أساسي **asāsī** *basic* 37

أسبوع أسابيع **usbū9 asābī9** *week* 44, 60

أستاذ أساتذة **ustā<u>dh</u> asāti<u>dh</u>a** *professor* 34

استثمار **isti<u>th</u>mār** *investment* 50

استخدام **isti<u>kh</u>dām** *employment, recruitment* 70

استعمال **isti9māl** *use* 50

استقبال **istiqbāl** *reception* 50, 70

استقلال **istiqlāl** *independence* 50, 71

استكشاف **istik<u>sh</u>āf** *exploration* 50

استنكار **istinkār** *rejection* 50

إسرائيل **isrā'īl** *Israel* 61

إسرائيلي **isrā'īlī** *Israeli* 37

أسس → أساس

أسعار → سعر

الإسكندرية **al-'iskandarīya** *Alexandria* 118

اسكوتلندا **iskotlanda** *Scotland* 54

اسم اسماء **ism asmā'** *name* 29

اسماء → اسم

أسواق → سوق

أسئلة → سؤال

إشارة **i<u>sh</u>āra** *sign* 91

اشرب **i<u>sh</u>rab** *drink!* 94

اشتراك **i<u>sh</u>tirāk** *participation* 70

اشتراكي **ishtirākī** *socialist* 70

اشتراكية **ishtirākīya** *socialism* 70

أشغال ← شغل

أشكال ← شكل

أشهر ← شهر

أشياء ← شيء

إصدار **iṣdār** *issue* 73

إصلاح **iṣlāḥ** *reform* 71

أصوات ← صوت

إضراب **iḍrāb** *strike* 35, 70

أطبّاء ← طبيب

اطلب **uṭlub** *ask for...!* 94

إعلان **i9lān** *announcement, notice, advertisement* 73

أعمال ← عمل

أغسطس **aghusṭus** *August* 115

افتح **iftaḥ** *open!* 94

أفلام ← فلم

اقتراح **iqtirāḥ** *proposal* 50, 55

اقتصاد **iqtiṣād** *economy, economics* 99

أقسام ← قسم

اقفل **iqfil** *shut!* 94

أقلاّء ← قليل

أكتوبر **oktōbir** *October* 116

أكثر **akthar** *more* 50, 55

آلات **ālāt** *tools* 15

ألف **alf** *thousand* 111

الآن **al-'ān** *now* 24

ألله **allāh** *God* 27

ألماني **almānī** *German* 16

ألمانيا **almāniya** *Germany* 36

ألوان ← لون

إلي **ila** *to* 52, 91

الإمارات (العربية المتحدة) **al-'imārāt (al-9arabīya l-muttaḥida)** *(United Arab) Emirates* 118

أمام **amām** *in front of* 15, 91

أمتار ← متر

إمكانية **imkānīya** *possibility* 50

أميركا **amayrka** *America* 61

أميركان ← أميركي

أميركي أميركان\أميركيون\...يين **amayrkī amayrkān/amayrkīyūn/-īyīn** *American* 61

أنا **ana** *I* 9, 85

أنباء ← نبأ

أنت **anta, anti** *you* 9, 85

إنتاج **intāj** *production* 41

انتباه **intibāh** *caution* 27

انتخاب **intikhāb** *election* 41, 70

انتظار **intiẓār** *wait(ing)* 70, 95

انتقال **intiqāl** *transfer* 71

أنتم **antum** *you* 16, 85

إنجليز → إنجليزي

إنجليزي إنجليز **ingilīzī ingilīz** *English, British* 60

انزل **inzil** *get off!* 94

أنصاف → نصف

انظر **unẓur** *see...!* 94

اهتمام **ihtimām** *attention* 27

أو **ow** *or* 18

أوتوبيس **otobīs** *bus* 54

أوتيل **ōtēl** *hotel* 54

أوطان → وطن

أوقات → وقت

أوّل **awwal** *first* 18, 112

أولى **ūla** *first* 112

أيّام → يوم

إيران **īrān** *Iran* 33

إيراني **īrānī** *Iranian* 36

إيطالي **īṭālī** *Italian* 58

إيطاليا **īṭāliya** *Italy* 42

إيقاف **īqāf** *parking* 91

أيار **ayār** *May* 115

أيلول **aylūl** *September* 115

أين **ayna** *where* 11

ب

ب **bi-** *with, by, in* 25, 91

باب أبواب **bāb abwāb** *door* 7

باريس **pārīs** *Paris* 54

باص **bāṣ** *bus* 35

باكستان **pākistān** *Pakistan* 61

البحر الأبيض المتوسّط **al-baḥr al-'abyaḍ al-mutawassiṭ** *Mediterranean Sea* 118

البحر الأحمر **al-baḥr al-'aḥmar** *Red Sea* 118

البحرين **al-baḥrayn** *Bahrain* 118

بدون **bidūn** *without* 91

برلمان **barlamān** *parliament* 92

بريد **barīd** *mail* 73

بريطانيا **barīṭāniya** *Britain* 42

بطالة **baṭāla** *unemployment* 84

بعد **ba9d** *after* 91; بعد الظّهر **ba9d aẓ-ẓuhr** *afternoon, p.m.* 109

بغداد **baghdād** *Baghdad* 118

بلاد → بلد

بلاد بلدان **bilād buldān** *country* 73

بلد بلاد **balad bilād** *town* 91

بلدان → بلاد

بلدية **baladīya** *town hall* 92

بنات → بنت

بنت بنات **bint banāt** *girl, daughter* 8

بنك بنوك **bank bunūk** *bank* 49, 60

بنوك → بنك

بوليس **būlīs** *police* 91

بيت بيوت **bayt buyūt** *house* 9, 60

بيروت **bayrūt** *Beirut* 118

بيضاء → دار

بيوت → بيت

ت

تاجر تجّار **tājir tujjār** *trader* 84

تاريخ تواريخ **tārīkh tawārīkh** *date* 109

تاسع **tāsi9** *ninth* 113

تأسيس **ta'sīs** *foundation* 29

تأمين **ta'mīn** *insurance* 99

تجّار → تاجر

تجارة **tijāra** *trade* 73

تجديد **tajdīd** *renewal* 71

تحت **taḥt** *below, under* 91

تحسين **taḥsīn** *repair* 50

تدخين **tadkhīn** *smoking* 91

تدريس **tadrīs** *instruction* 71

تربية **tarbiya** *education* 99

تسجيل **tasjīl** *registration* 99

تسعة **tis9a** *nine* 110

تشرين الأوّل **tishrīn al-'awwal** *October* 116

تشرين الثاني **tishrīn ath-thānī** *November* 116

تعليم **ta9līm** *tuition, education* 50, 69

تعليمي **ta9līmī** *educational, tutorial* 70

تفتيش **taftīsh** *inspection* 48, 69

تقديم **taqdīm** *presentation* 73

تقارير → تقرير

تقرير **taqrīr** *decision* 49, 61, 69

تقرير تقارير **taqrīr taqārīr** *report* 49, 61, 69

تقسيم **taqsīm** *partition* 50

تكاليف → تكليف

تكليف تكاليف **taklīf takālīf** *cost* 50

تلّ تلال **tall tilāl** *hill* 19

تلال → تلّ

تلفون **tilifōn** *telephone* 54

تليفزيون **tilivizyūn** *television* 73

تليفون **tilīfōn** *telephone* 54

تمام **tamām** *perfect* 16

تمهّل **tamahhal** *slow down!* 27, 94

تمّوز **tammūz** *July* 115

تمويل **tamwīl** *financing* 17, 71

تنبّؤ **tanabbu'** *forecast* 24

تنبيه **tanbīh** *warning* 27

تنظيم **tanẓīm** *organisation* 42, 69

تواريخ → تاريخ

توقيف **touqīf** *parking* 91

تونس **tūnis** *Tunis(ia)* 118

ث

ثابت **thābit** *firm, solid* 7

ثالث **thālith** *third* 14, 112

ثامن **thāmin** *eighth* 113

ثانوي **thānawī** *secondary* 17

ثاني **thānī** *second* 112

ثاني عشر **thānī 9ashar** *twelfth* 113

ثلاث\ثلاثة **thalāth(a)** *three* 15, 110

الثلاثاء **ath-thalātha** *Tuesday* 115

ثلث أثلاث **thulth athlāth** *a third* 113

ثمانية **thamāniya** *eight* 110

ثنائي **thunā'ī** *double* 24

ج

چاكارتا **jakārta** *Jakarta* 54

جامعة **jāmi9a** *university* 92

جدد → جديد

جديد جدد **jadīd judud** *new* 73

جرائد → جريدة

جراچ **garāj** *garage* 91

جريدة جرائد **jarīda jarā'id** *newspaper* 74

الجزائر **al-jazā'ir** *Algeria, Algiers* 118

جمادى الآخرة **jumāda l-'ākhira** see 116

جمادى الأولى **jumāda l-'ūla** see 116

جمرك **jumruk** *customs* 99

الجمعة **al-jum9a** *Friday* 115

جميل **jamīl** *beautiful* 73

جنوب **janūb** *south* 41

جنوبي **janūbī** *southern* 41

جنيف **jinēv** *Geneva* 54

جنيه **jinayh** *pound (£)* 109

جوّي **jawwī**
air (adjective) 73

ح

حادى عشر **ḥādī 9ashar**
eleventh 113

حاضر **ḥāḍir**
present, ready 67

حدّ حدود **ḥadd ḥudūd**
limit 91

حداث ← حديث

حدود ← حدّ

حديث حداث **ḥadīth ḥidāth**
modern 73

حزيران **ḥazīrān** *June* 115

حساب **ḥisāb** *account* 99

حسب **ḥasab**
according to 91

حكومة **ḥukūma**
government 73

خ

خارج **khārij** *outside* 91

خارجية **khārijīya**
Foreign Affairs 99

خاصّ **khāṣṣ** *private, special, particular* 41

خاصّةً **khāṣṣatan**
specially 51

خامس **khāmis** *fifth* 113

خبر أخبار **khabar akhbār**
news item 41, 59

خبراء ← خبير

خبير خبراء **khabīr khubarā’**
expert 84

الخرطوم **al-kharṭūm**
Khartoum 118

خروج **khurūj** *exit* 41

خطّ خطوط **khaṭṭ khuṭūṭ**
line 42, 60

خطاب أخطبة **khiṭāb akhṭiba**
speech 73

خطر أخطار **khaṭar akhṭār**
danger 42, 59

خطر **khaṭir** *dangerous* 42

خطوط ← خطّ

خلال **khilāl** *during* 91

الخليج (العربي) **al-khalīj (al-9arabī)**
(Arabian) Gulf 118

خمسة **khamsa** *five* 110

الخميس **al-khamīs**
Thursday 115

خياطة **khiyāṭa** *sewing* 62

د

داخل **dākhil** *inside* 91

داخلية **dākhilīya**
Home Affairs 99

الدار البيضاء **ad-dār al-bayḍā’**
Casablanca 118

دائرة دوائر **dā'ira dawā'ir** *directorate* 34, 99

دبيّ **dubayy** *Dubai* 118

دخول **dukhūl** *entry* 41

دراسة **dirāsa** *study* 34

دراسي **dirāsī** *academic* 37

دراهم → درهم

درهم دراهم **dirham darāhim** *dirham* 109

دسمبر **disambir** *December* 116

دفاع **difā9** *defence* 99

دفع مدفوعات **daf9 madfū9āt** *payment* 99

دقائق → دقيقة

دقيقة دقائق **daqīqa daqā'iq** *minute* 109

دمشق **dimashq** *Damascus* 118

دموقراطية **dimuqrāṭīya** *democracy* 70

دنانير → دينار

دوائر → دائرة

الدّوحة **ad-douḥa** *Doha* 118

دولار **dōlār** *dollar* 109

دولي **duwalī** *international* 84

دون **dūn** *without* 91

دينار دنانير **dīnār danānīr** *dinar* 109

ذ

ذو الحجّة **dhu l-ḥijja** see 116

ذو القعدة **dhu l-qa9da** see 116

ر

رابع **rābi9** *fourth* 113

راتب رواتب **rātib rawātib** *salary* 84

راديو **rādiō** *radio* 73

الرّباط **ar-ribāṭ** *Rabat* 118

ربع أرباع **rub9 arbā9** *a quarter* 113

ربيع الأوّل **rabī9 al-'awwal** see 116

ربيع الثّاني **rabī9 ath-thānī** see 116

الرجاء **ar-rajā'** *please...* 95

رجب **rajab** see 116

رخص → رخصة

رخصة رخص **rukhṣa rukhaṣ** *licence* 99

رسالة **risāla** *letter* 73

رسمي **rasmī** *official* 73

رسمياً **rasmīyan** *officially* 51

رقم أرقام **raqm arqām** *number* 49

رمضان **ramaḍān** see 116

رواتب → راتب

رؤساء ← رئيس
روما rōma *Rome* 54
الرّياض ar-riyāḍ *Riyadh* 118
ريال riyāl *rial, riyal* 33
رئيس رؤساء ra'īs ru'asā' *chairman, chief, president, head* 33
رئيسي ra'īsī *main, principal* 37

ز

زائر زوّار zā'ir zuwwār *visitor* 62
زراعة zirā9a *agriculture* 99
زملاء ← زميل
زميل زملاء zamīl zumalā' *colleague* 73
زوّار ← زائر
زيارة ziyāra *visit* 33

س

سابع sābi9 *seventh* 113
سادس sādis *sixth* 113
سادة ← سيّد
ساعة sā9a *hour* 109
ساكن سكّان sākin sukkān *resident* 50
سائق sā'iq *driver* 50, 67, 68
سباكة sibāka *plumbing* 62
السّبت as-sabt *Saturday* 115
سبتمبر sibtambir *September* 115
سبعة sab9a *seven* 110
ستّة sitta *six* 110
سرعة sur9a *speed* 91
سعر أسعار si9r as9ār *price* 44, 59
سفراء ← سفير
سفارة sifāra *embassy* 48
سفير سفراء safīr sufarā' *ambassador* 48
سكّان ← ساكن
سلام salām *peace* 93
سماسير ← سمسار
سمسار سماسير simsār samāsīr *broker* 84
سنة سنوات sana sanawāt *year* 29, 109
سنوات ← سنة
السّعودية as-sa9ūdīya *Saudi Arabia* 118
السّودان as-sūdān *Sudan* 118
سؤال أسئلة su'āl as'ila *question* 29
سوري sūrī *Syrian* 36
سوريا sūriya *Syria* 36

سوق أسواق **sūq aswāq** (f.) *market* 49

سويسرا **swisira** *Switzerland* 54

سياحة **siyāḥa** *tourism* 62

سيّارة **sayyāra** *car* 33

سياسة **siyāsa** *policy, politics* 99

سيّد سادة **sayyid sāda** *Mr, gentleman* 34

سيّدة **sayyida** *Mrs, lady* 34

ش

شارع **shāri9 shawāri9** *street* 44

شاي **shāy** *tea* 29

شباط **shubāṭ** *February* 115

شخصي **shakhṣī** *personal* 73

شرطة **shurṭa** *police* 42

شرطي **shurṭī** *policeman* 92

شرق **sharq** *east* 49

شركة **sharika** *company* 49

شعبان **sha9bān** see 116

شغل أشغال **shughl ashghāl** *work, job* 84

شكل أشكال **shakl ashkāl** *form* 50, 55

شمال **shimāl** *north* 29

شمالي **shimālī** *northern* 29

شمس **shams** *sun* 29

شهر أشهر **shahr ashhur** *month* 33, 109

شوارع ← شارع

شوّال **shawwāl** see 116

شيء أشياء **shay' ashyā'** *thing* 29, 59

ص

صباح **ṣabāḥ** *morning* 109

صباحًا **ṣabāḥan** *a.m.* 109

صحافة **ṣiḥāfa** *press* 73

صحف ← صحيفة

صحفي **ṣuḥufī** *journalist* 73

صحيفة صحف **ṣaḥīfa ṣuḥuf** *newspaper* 73

صرّاف **ṣarrāf** *money changer* 109

صرف **ṣarf** *exchange* 109

صعاب ← صعب

صعب صعاب **ṣa9b ṣi9āb** *difficult* 84

صغار ← صغير

صغير صغار **ṣaghīr ṣighār** *small* 50

صفر **ṣifr** *zero* 109; **ṣafar** see 116

صناعة **ṣinā9a** *industry* 44

صوت أصوات **ṣowt aṣwāt** *voice* 35

صور ← صورة

صورة صور **ṣūra ṣuwar** *picture, photograph* 73

ض

ضدّ **ḍidd** *against* 91

ضرائب ← ضريبة

ضرورة **ḍarūra** *necessity* 35

ضروري **ḍarūrī** *necessary* 36

ضريبة ضرائب **ḍarība ḍarā'ib** *tax* 99

ط

طالب طلاّب **ṭālib ṭullāb** *student* 68

طائرة **ṭā'ira** *aeroplane* 42

طبيب أطبّاء **ṭabīb aṭibbā'** *doctor* 84

طرابلس **ṭarābulus** *Tripoli* 118

طرق ← طريق

طريق طرق **ṭarīq ṭuruq** *road* 91

طلاّب ← طالب

طوال ← طويل

طويل طوال **ṭawīl ṭiwāl** *long* 73

ظ

ظهر **ẓuhr** *midday* 109

ع

عادةً **9ādatan** *usually* 51

عارف **9ārif** *knowing* 68

عاشر **9āshir** *tenth* 113

عاصمة عواصم **9āṣima 9awāṣim** *capital city* 92

عالم عوالم **9ālam 9awālim** *world* 118

عالمي **9ālamī** *world(wide)* 84

عامل عمّال **9āmil 9ummāl** *worker, workman* 50, 62, 67

عامّ **9āmm** *general, public* 44

عدم **9adam** *lack* 95; الرجاء عدم **ar-rajā' 9adam** *please do not...* 95

العراق **al-9irāq** *Iraq* 49

عراقي **9irāqī** *Iraqi* 87

عرب ← عربي

عربي عرب **9arabī 9arab** *Arab* 60

عشرة 9ashra *ten* 110
عقد عقود 9aqd 9uqūd *contract* 99
عقود → عقد
علاقات 9alāqāt *relations* 73
على 9ala *on* 52, 91
عمّال → عامل
عمان 9umān *Oman* 118
عمّان 9ammān *Amman* 118
عمل أعمال 9amal a9māl *work, labour* 69, 84
عن 9an *from, about* 91
عواصم → عاصمة

غ

غائب ghā'ib *absent* 84
غرب gharb *west* 44
غربي gharbī *western* 44
غير ghayr *apart from* 92

ف

فبراير fibrāyir *February* 115
فقراء → فقير
فقير فقراء faqīr fuqarā' *poor* 50
فلسطين filasṭīn *Palestine* 118
فلم أفلام film aflām *film* 59
فلوس fulūs *money* 109
فنّي fannī *technical* 48
فوراً fouran *immediately* 51
فوق fouq *above, over* 92
في fī *in* 91
فيينا\ڤيينا viyēna *Vienna* 54

ق

القاهرة al-qāhira *Cairo* 49
قبل qabl *before* 91
القدس al-quds *Jerusalem* 118
قراءة qirā'a (act of) *reading* 73
قريب qarīb *near* 50
قسم أقسام qism aqsām *department* 99
قصار → قصير
قصر قصور qaṣr quṣūr *palace* 92
قصور → قصر
قصير قصار qaṣīr qiṣār *short* 73
قطر qaṭar *Qatar* 118
قف qif *Stop!* 49, 94
قليل أقلاّء qalīl aqillā' *little, few* 50
قليلاً qalīlan *a little* 51
قنصلية qunṣulīya *consulate* 92

ك

ك **ka-** *like, as* 92

كاتب كتّاب **kātib kuttāb** *writer, clerk* 50, 62, 67

كامل كملة **kamil kamala** *complete* 68

كانون الأوّل **kānūn al-'awwal** *December* 116

كانون الثاني **kānūn ath-thānī** *January* 115

كبار ← كبير

كبير كبار **kabīr kibār** *big* 49

كتّاب ← كاتب

كتابة **kitāba** (act of) *writing* 69

كثير **kathīr** *much* 50

كثيراً **kathīran** *greatly* 51

كراج **garāj** *garage* 91

كلّ **kull** *every, all* 50

كلام **kalām** *speech, speaking* 50

كمبيوتر **kampyūtir** *computer* 54

كملة ← كامل

كمّية **kammīya** *quantity* 50, 55

الكويت **al-kuwayt** *Kuwait* 65, 118

كيلومتر **kīlomitr** *kilometre* 91

ل

ل **li-** *to, for, of* 25, 91

لا **la** *no* 15

لازم **lāzim** *necessary* 67

لبنان **lubnān** *Lebanon* 14

لبناني **lubnānī** *Lebanese* 14

لتر **litr** *litre* 33

لجان ← لجنة

لجنة لجان **lajna lijān** *committee* 41

لغة **lugha** *language* 73

لمّا **lamma** *when* 19

لمن **li-man** *whose* 19

لون ألوان **loun alwān** *colour* 17

لي **lī** *to/for me* 14

ليبي **lībī** *Libyan* 16

ليبيا **lībiya** *Libya* 36

ليرة **līra** *lira* 33

م

مارس **māris** *March* 115

مالية **mālīya** *Financial Affairs* 99

مأمور **ma'mūr** *public official* 84

مائة **mīya** *hundred* 111

مايو **māyū** *May* 17, 115

مبالغ ← مبلغ

مبروك **mabrūk** *Congratulations* 121

مبلغ مبالغ **mablagh mabāligh** *sum* 44

متاحف ← متحف

متّحد **muttaḥid** *united* 68, 118

متحف متاحف **matḥaf matāḥif** *museum* 50

متر أمتار **mitr amtār** *metre* 33

متوسّط ← بحر

مثل **mithl** *like, as* 19, 92

مثلاً **mathalan** *for example* 51

مجالس ← مجلس

مجتهد **mujtahid** *hardworking* 73

مجلس مجالس **majlis majālis** *council* 92

مجلّة **majalla** *magazine* 73

محاسب **muḥāsib** *accountant* 67

محاسبات **muḥāsabāt** *accounts* 69

محافظ **muḥāfiẓ** *conservative* 68

محاكم ← محكمة

محامي **muḥāmī** *lawyer* 67

محتلّ **muḥtall** *occupied* 118

محرّك **muḥarrik** *engine* 50

محرّم **muḥarram** see 116

محفوظ **maḥfūẓ** *reserved* 67

محكمة محاكم **maḥkama maḥākim** *law-court* 62

محلّي **maḥallī** *local* 73

مخارج ← مخرج

مخرج مخارج **makhraj makhārij** *exit* 41, 60

مدّة مدد **mudda mudad** *period* 109

مداخل ← مدخل

مدارس ← مدرسة

مدخل مداخل **madkhal madākhil** *entrance* 41, 60

مدد ← مدّة

مدراء ← مدير

مدرّس **mudarris** *instructor* 50, 67

مدرسة مدارس **madrasa madāris** *school* 34, 60, 62

مدفوعات ← دفع

مدني **madanī** *civil, urban* 84

مدير مدراء **mudīr mudarā'** *director* 34, 60

مدن ← مدينة

مدينة مدن **madīna mudun** *city* 91

مراسل **murāsil** *correspondent* 73

مراكز → مركز

مربوط **marbūṭ** *connected* 50

مرسل **mursil** *sender* 67; **mursal** *sent* 67

مرّة **marra** *a time* 33

مرضى → مريض

مركز مراكز **markaz marākiz** *centre* 92

مرور **murūr** *traffic* 33, *passing, turning* 91

مريض مرضى **marīḍ marḍa** *sick* 35

مساعد **musā9id** *assistant* 67

مساعدة **musā9ada** *help* 69

مسافر **musāfir** *traveller* 67

مستأجر **musta'jir** *tenant* 68

مستثمر **mustathmir** *investor* 68

مستخدم **mustakhdim** *employer* 68; **mustakhdam** *employed* 68

مستشفى **mustashfa** *hospital* 52

مستعدّ **musta9idd** *ready* 68

مستعمل **musta9mil** *user* 68

مستقبل **mustaqbil** *(radio, (radio, TV) receiver* 68; **mustaqbal** *future* 68

مستنكر **mustankar** *rejected* 68

مسرور **masrūr** *pleased* 33

مسقط **masqaṭ** *Muscat* 118

مسلّح **musallaḥ** *armed* 68

مسؤول **mas'ūl** *responsible* 29

مشاغل → مشغل

مشاكل → مشكلة

مشترك **mushtarik** *participant* 68; **mushtarak** *joint, common* 68

مشغل مشاغل **mashghal mashāghil** *workshop* 50

مشغول **mashghūl** *busy* 44, 67

مشكلة مشاكل **mushkila mashākil** *problem* 50, 60

مشهور **mashhūr** *famous* 84

مصارف → مصرف

مصانع → مصنع

مصر **miṣr** *Egypt* 35

مصرف مصارف **maṣrif maṣārif** *bank* 109

مصري **miṣrī** *Egyptian* 37
مصنع مصانع **maṣna9 maṣāni9** *factory* 50
مطبخ ← مطابخ
مطار **maṭār** *airport* 42
مطعم ← مطاعم
مطبخ مطابخ **maṭbakh maṭābikh** *kitchen* 50
مطبوع **maṭbū9** *printed* 62
مطعم مطاعم **maṭ9am maṭā9im** *restaurant* 44
مع **ma9** *with* 91
معرض ← معارض
معرض معارض **ma9riḍ ma9āriḍ** *exhibition* 73
معروف **ma9rūf** *known* 62
معطي **mu9ṭī** *donor* 67
معقول **ma9qūl** *reasonable* 84
معلّم **mu9allim** *teacher* 44, 67
معلّمة **mu9allima** *teacher* 68
معلوم **ma9lūm** *known* 50
معلومات **ma9lūmāt** *information* 67
مغادرة **mughādara** *departure* 69
المغرب **al-maghrib** *Morocco* 118
مفتاح ← مفاتيح
مفرق ← مفارق
مفتاح مفاتيح **miftāḥ mafātīḥ** *key* 50, 60
مفتّش **mufattish** *inspector* 50, 67
مفتوح **maftūḥ** *open* 49, 67
مفرق مفارق **mafraq mafāriq** *crossroad* 91
مفيد **mufīd** *useful* 67
مقابل **muqābil** *facing* 68
مقالة **maqāla** (press) *article* 73
مقبول **maqbūl** *acceptable* 84
مقترح **muqtaraḥ** *proposed* 68
مقرّر **muqarrir** *reporter* 50, 67; **muqarrar** *decided* 67
مكتب\مكتبة ← مكاتب
مكتب مكاتب **maktab makātib** *office* 49, 60
مكتبة مكاتب **maktaba makātib** *library, bookshop* 62
مكتوب **maktūb** *written* 50, 62, 67
مكتوم **maktūm** *confidential* 62

مكسور **maksūr** *broken* 68

ملابس **malābis** *clothes* 29

ملاعب → ملعب

ملايين → مليون

ملعب ملاعب **mal9ab malā9ib** *playground, playing-field* 50

ملوّن **mulawwan** *coloured* 73

مليون ملايين **milyūn malāyīn** *million* 111

ممتاز **mumtāz** *excellent* 73

ممثّل **muma<u>thth</u>il** *representative* 18, 67; **muma<u>thth</u>al** *represented* 67

ممرّض\ممرّضة **mumarriḍ(a)** *nurse* 84

ممكن **mumkin** *possible* 49

ممنوع **mamnū9** *prohibited* 62, 67, 91

ممنون **mamnūn** *grateful* 17

من **min** *from* 15, 91

مناسب **munāsib** *appropriate* 67

مناسبة **munāsaba** *occasion* 71

منتخب **munta<u>kh</u>ib** *elector* 68; **munta<u>kh</u>ab** *elected* 68

منتظر **muntaẓir** *waiting for* 68; **muntaẓar** *awaited* 68

مندوب **mandūb** *delegate* 73

منشور **man<u>sh</u>ūr** *published* 50

منظّمة **munaẓẓama** *organisation* 42

مهمّ **muhimm** *important* 67

مهندس **muhandis** *engineer* 84

مواصلات **muwāṣalāt** *communications* 73

موت **mowt** *death* 19

مؤتمر **mu'tamar** *conference* 73

موجود **moujūd** *present* (not absent) 84

موريتانية **mūrītāniya** *Mauritania* 118

موظّف **muwaẓẓaf** *employee* 84

ميلادية **mīlādīya** *AD* 116

مئة **mīya** *hundred* 111

ميادين → ميدان

ميدان ميادين **maydān mayādīn** *square* 91

ن

نائب نوّاب **nā'ib nuwwāb** *deputy* 62

نائم **nā'im** *asleep* 24

نبأ أنباء **naba' anbā'** *news item* 24, 59

نبات **nabāt** *vegetation* 9

نجارة **nijāra** *carpentry* 62

نحن **naḥnu** *we* 85

نصّ نصوص **naṣṣ nuṣūṣ** *text* 73

نصف أنصاف **niṣf anṣāf** *half* 113

نصوص ← نصّ

نفط **nafṭ** *oil* 99

نقل **naql** *transport* 91

نقود **nuqūd** *money* 109

نمر ← نمرة

نمرة نمر **numra numar** *number* 99

نمل **naml** *ants* 16

نهائي **nihā'ī** *final* 27

نوّاب ← نائب

نوفمبر **nūfimbir** *November* 116

نيسان **nīsān** *April* 115

نيل **nīl** *Nile* 20

هـ

هامّ **hāmm** *important* 27

هجرية **hijrīya** *AH* 116

هم **hum** *they* 27, 85

هندسة **handasa** *engineering* 84

هندي هنود **hindī hunūd** *Indian* 60

هنود ← هندي

هو **huwa** *he* 27, 85

هي **hiya** *she* 27, 85

و

و **wa** *and* 17, 25

واحد **wāḥid** *one* 109

وارد **wārid** *arriving* 68

واضح **wāḍiḥ** *clear* 84

وراء **warā'** *behind* 92

وزارة **wizāra** *ministry* 33

وزراء ← وزير

وزير وزراء **wazīr wuzarā'** *minister* 60

وصول **wuṣūl** *arrival* 35, 69

وطن أوطان **waṭan owṭān** *nation* 42

وطني **waṭanī** *national* 42

وظائف ← وظيفة

وظيفة وظائف **waẓīfa waẓā'if** *job, post* 84

وقت أوقات **waqt owqāt** *time* 109

وقوف **wuqūf** *stopping* 91

وكالة **wikāla** *agency* 84

وكلاء → وكيل

وكيل وكلاء **wakīl wukalā'** *agent* 84

ي

اليابان **al-yābān** *Japan* 19

ياباني **yābānī** *Japanese* 10

يسار **yasār** *left(-hand)* 91

اليمن **al-yaman** *Yemen* 118

يمين **yamīn** *right(-hand)* 91

يناير **yanāyir** *January* 115

يهود → يهودي

يهودي يهود **yahūdī yahūd** *Jew(ish)* 60

يوليو **yūliyū** *July* 17, 115

يوم أيّام **youm ayyām** *day* 17, 109;

اليوم **al-youm** *today* 99

يونيو **yūniyū** *June* 17, 115

English-Arabic Vocabulary

This vocabulary does not list:

- the possessives, which can be found in Unit 9, the personal pronouns, which can be found in Unit 10, or the prepositions, which can be found in Unit 11,
- numbers, days of the week or names of the months, which can all be found in Unit 13.

A

absent غائب **ghā'ib** 84

Abu Dhabi أبو ظبي **abū ẓabī** 118

academic دراسي **dirāsī** 37

acceptable مقبول **maqbūl** 84

account حساب **ḥisāb** 99

accountant محاسب **muḥāsib** 67

accounts محاسبات **muḥāsabāt** 69

administration إدارة **idāra** 34, 70

advertisement إعلان **i9lān** 73

aeroplane طائرة **ṭā'ira** 42

afternoon بعد الظهر **ba9d aẓ-ẓuhr** 109

agency وكالة **wikāla** 84

agent وكيل وكلاء **wakīl wukalā'** 84

agriculture زراعة **zirā9a** 99

air (adjective) جوي **jawwī** 73

airport مطار **maṭār** 42

Alexandria الإسكندرية **al-'iskandarīya** 118

Algeria, Algiers الجزائر **al-jazā'ir** 118

all كلّ **kull** 50

a.m. صباحًا **ṣabāḥan** 109

ambassador سفير سفراء **safīr sufarā'** 48

America أميركا **amayrka** 61

American أميركي أميركان\ أميركيون\...يين **amayrkī amayrkān/ amayrkīyūn/-īyīn** 61

Amman عمّان **9ammān** 118

and و **wa** 17, 25

announcement إعلان **i9lān** 73

ants نمل **naml** 16

appropriate مناسب **munāsib** 67

Arab عربي عرب **9arabī 9arab** 60

armed مسلّح **musallaḥ** 68

arrival وصول **wuṣūl** 35, 69

arriving وارد **wārid** 68
(press) *article* مقالة **maqāla** 73
ask for…! اطلب **uṭlub** 94
asleep نائم **nā'im** 24
assistant مساعد **musā9id** 67
attention اهتمام **ihtimām** 27
awaited منتظر **muntaẓar** 68

B

Baghdad بغداد **baghdād** 118
Bahrain البحرين **al-baḥrayn** 118
bank بنك بنوك **bank bunūk** 49, 60; مصرف مصارف **maṣrif maṣārif** 109
basic أساسي **asāsī** 37
basis أساس أسس **asās usus** 29
beautiful جميل **jamīl** 73
beginning ابتداء **ibtidā'** 34
Beirut بيروت **bayrūt** 118
big كبير كبار **kabīr kibār** 49
bookshop مكتبة مكاتب **maktaba makātib** 62
Britain بريطانيا **barīṭāniya** 42
British إنجليزي إنجليز **ingilīzī ingilīz** 60
broken مكسور **maksūr** 68
broker سمسار سماسير **simsār samāsīr** 84
bus باص **bāṣ** 35; أوتوبيس **otobīs** 54
busy مشغول **mashghūl** 44, 67

C

Cairo القاهرة **al-qāhira** 49
camels إبل **ibil** 14
capital city عاصمة عواصم **9āṣima 9awāṣim** 92
car سيّارة **sayyāra** 33
carpentry نجارة **nijāra** 62
Casablanca الدار البيضاء **ad-dār al-bayḍā'** 118
caution انتباه **intibāh** 27
centre مركز مراكز **markaz marākiz** 92
chairman, chief رئيس رؤساء **ra'īs ru'asā'** 33
city مدينة مدن **madīna mudun** 91
civil مدني **madanī** 84
clear واضح **wāḍiḥ** 84
clerk كاتب كتّاب **kātib kuttāb** 67
clothes ملابس **malābis** 29
colleague زميل زملاء **zamīl zumalā'** 73

colour لون ألوان **loun alwān** 17

coloured ملوّن **mulawwan** 73

committee لجنة لجان **lajna lijān** 41

common مشترك **mushtarak** 68

communications مواصلات **muwāṣalāt** 73

company شركة **sharika** 49

complete كامل كملة **kāmil kamala** 68

computer كمبيوتر **kampyūtir** 54

conference مؤتمر **mu'tamar** 73

confidential مكتوم **maktūm** 62

Congratulations مبروك **mabrūk** 121

connected مربوط **marbūṭ** 50

conservative محافظ **muḥāfiẓ** 68

consulate قنصلية **qunṣulīya** 92

contract عقد عقود **9aqd 9uqūd** 99

correspondent مراسل **murāsil** 73

cost تكليف تكاليف **taklīf takālīf** 50

council مجلس مجالس **majlis majālis** 92

country بلاد بلدان **bilād buldān** 73

crossroad مفرق مفارق **mafraq mafāriq** 91

customs جمرك **jumruk** 99

D

Damascus دمشق **dimashq** 118

danger خطر أخطار **khaṭar akhṭār** 42, 59

dangerous خطر **khaṭir** 42

date تاريخ تواريخ **tārīkh tawārīkh** 109

daughter بنت بنات **bint banāt** 8

day يوم أيّام **youm ayyām** 17, 109

death موت **mowt** 19

decided مقرّر **muqarrar** 67

decision تقرير **taqrīr** 49, 61, 69

defence دفاع **difā9** 99

delegate مندوب **mandūb** 73

democracy دموقراطية **dimuqrāṭīya** 70

department قسم أقسام **qism aqsām** 99

departure مغادرة **mughādara** 69

deputy نائب نوّاب **nā'ib nuwwāb** 62

despatch إرسال **irsāl** 70

difficult صعب صعاب **ṣa9b ṣi9āb** 84

dinar دينار دنانير **dīnār danānīr** 109

director مدير مدراء **mudīr mudarā'** 34, 60

directorate دائرة دوائر **dā'ira dawā'ir** 34, 99

dirham درهم دراهم **dirham darāhim** 109

doctor طبيب أطبّاء **ṭabīb aṭibbā'** 84

Doha الدّوحة **ad-douḥa** 118

dollar دولار **dōlār** 109

donor معطي **mu9ṭī** 67

door باب أبواب **bāb abwāb** 7

double ثنائي **thunā'ī** 24

drink! اشرب **ishrab** 94

driver سائق **sā'iq** 50, 67

Dubai دبي **dubayy** 118

E

east شرق **sharq** 49

economics, economy اقتصاد **iqtiṣād** 99

education تعليم **ta9līm** 69; تربية **tarbiya** 99

educational تعليمي **ta9līmī** 70

Egypt مصر **miṣr** 35

Egyptian مصري **miṣrī** 37

elected منتخب **muntakhab** 68

election انتخاب **intikhāb** 41, 70

elector منتخب **muntakhib** 68

embassy سفارة **sifāra** 48

Emirates (United Arab) الإمارات (العربية المتّحدة) **al-'imārāt (al-9arabīya l-muttaḥida)** 118

employed مستخدم **mustakhdam** 68

employee موظّف **muwaẓẓaf** 84

employer مستخدم **mustakhdim** 68

employment استخدام **istikhdām** 70

engine محرك **muḥarrik** 50

engineer مهندس **muhandis** 84

engineering هندسة **handasa** 84

English إنجليزي إنجليز **ingilīzī ingilīz** 60

entrance مدخل مداخل **madkhal madākhil** 41, 60

entry دخول **dukhūl** 41

every كلّ **kull** 50

for example مثلاً **mathalan** 51

excellent ممتاز **mumtāz** 73

exchange صرف **ṣarf** 109

exhibition معرض معارض **ma9riḍ ma9āriḍ** 73

exit خروج **khurūj** 41; مخرج مخارج **makhraj makhārij** 41, 60

expert خبير خبراء **khabīr khubarā'** 84

exploration استكشاف **istikshāf** 50

F

facing مقابل **muqābil** 68

factory مصنع مصانع **maṣna9 maṣāni9** 50

famous مشهور **mashhūr** 84

father أب آباء **ab ābā'** 7

few قليل أقلاّء **qalīl aqillā'** 50

film فلم أفلام **film aflām** 59

final نهائي **nihā'ī** 27

Financial Affairs مالية **mālīya** 99

financing تمويل **tamwīl** 17, 71

firm ثابت **thābit** 7

forecast تنبّؤ **tanabbu'** 24

foreign أجنبي أجانب **ajnabī ajānib** 41, 73

Foreign Affairs خارجية **khārijīya** 99

form شكل أشكال **shakl ashkāl** 50, 55

foundation تأسيس **ta'sīs** 29

furniture أثاث **athāth** 7

future مستقبل **mustaqbal** 68

G

garage جراچ\كراج **garāj** 91

general عامّ **9āmm** 44

Geneva جنيف **jinēv** 54

gentleman سيّد سادة **sayyid sāda** 34

German ألماني **almānī** 16

Germany ألمانيا **almāniya** 36

get off! انزل **inzil** 94

get on! اركب **irkab** 94

girl بنت بنات **bint banāt** 8

God ألله **allāh** 27

government حكومة **ḥukūma** 73

grateful ممنون **mamnūn** 17

greatly كثيراً **kathīran** 51

(Arabian) Gulf الخليج (العربي) **al-khalīj (al-9arabī)** 118

H

hardworking مجتهد **mujtahid** 73

head رئيس رؤساء **ra'īs ru'asā'** 33

help مساعدة **musā9ada** 69

hill تلّ تلال **tall tilāl** 19

Home Affairs داخلية **dākhilīya** 99

hospital مستشفى **mustashfa** 52

hotel أوتيل **ōtēl** 54
hour ساعة **sā9a** 109
house بيت بيوت
bayt buyūt 9, 60

I

immediately فوراً **fouran** 51
important هامّ **hāmm** 27;
مهم **muhimm** 67
independence استقلال
istiqlāl 50, 71
Indian هندي هنود
hindī hunūd 60
industry صناعة **ṣinā9a** 44
information معلومات
ma9lūmāt 67
initial ابتدائي **ibtidā'ī** 37
inspection تفتيش **taftīsh** 48, 69
inspector مفتّش
mufattish 50, 67
instruction تدريس **tadrīs** 71
instructor مدرّس
mudarris 50, 67
insurance تأمين **ta'mīn** 99
international دولي **duwalī** 84
investment استثمار **istithmār** 50
investor مستثمر
mustathmir 68
Iran إيران **īrān** 33
Iranian إيراني **īrānī** 36
Iraq العراق **al-9irāq** 49
Iraqi عراقي **9irāqī** 87
Israel إسرائيل **isrā'īl** 61
Israeli إسرائيلي **isrā'īlī** 37
issue إصدار **iṣdār** 73
Italian إيطالي **īṭālī** 58
Italy إيطاليا **īṭāliya** 42

J

Japan اليابان **al-yābān** 19
Japanese ياباني **yābānī** 10
Jerusalem القدس **al-quds** 118
Jew(ish) يهودي يهود
yahūdī yahūd 60
job شغل أشغال
shughl ashghāl 84;
وظيفة وظائف
waẓīfa waẓā'if 84
joint مشترك **mushtarak** 68
Jordan الأردن **al-'urdun** 118
journalist صحفي **ṣuḥufi** 73

K

key مفتاح مفاتيح
miftāḥ mafātīḥ 50, 60
Khartoum الخرطوم **al-kharṭūm** 118
kilometre كيلومتر **kīlomitr** 91
kitchen مطبخ مطابخ
maṭbakh maṭābikh 50
knowing عارف **9ārif** 68

known معلوم **ma9lūm** 50; معروف **ma9rūf** 62
Kuwait الكويت **al-kuwayt** 118

L

labour عمل أعمال **9amal a9māl** 84
lack عدم **9adam** 95
lady سيّدة **sayyida** 34
language لغة **lugha** 73
law-court محكمة محاكم **maḥkama maḥākim** 62
lawyer محامي **muḥāmī** 67
Lebanese لبناني **lubnānī** 14
Lebanon لبنان **lubnān** 14
left(-hand) يسار **yasār** 91
letter رسالة **risāla** 73
library مكتبة مكاتب **maktaba makātib** 62
Libya ليبيا **lībiya** 36
Libyan ليبي **lībī** 16
licence رخصة رخص **rukhṣa rukhaṣ** 99
limit حدّ حدود **ḥadd ḥudūd** 91
line خطّ خطوط **khaṭṭ khuṭūṭ** 42, 60
lira ليرة **līra** 33
litre لتر **litr** 33
little قليل أقلاّء **qalīl aqillā'** 50
a little قليلاً **qalīlan** 51
local محلّي **maḥallī** 73
long طويل طوال **ṭawīl ṭiwāl** 73

M

magazine مجلّة **majalla** 73
mail بريد **barīd** 73
main رئيسي **ra'īsī** 37
market سوق أسواق **sūq aswāq** (f.) 49
Mauritania موريتانية **mūrītāniya** 118
Mediterranean Sea البحر الأبيض المتوسّط **al-baḥr al-'abyaḍ al-mutawassiṭ** 118
meeting اجتماع **ijtimā9** 44, 71
metre متر أمتار **mitr amtār** 33
midday ظهر **ẓuhr** 109
minister وزير وزراء **wazīr wuzarā'** 60
ministry وزارة **wizāra** 33
minute دقيقة دقائق **daqīqa daqā'iq** 109
modern حديث حداث **ḥadīth ḥidāth** 73

money فلوس **fulūs** 109; نقود **nuqūd** 109
money changer صراف **ṣarrāf** 109
month شهر أشهر **shahr ashhur** 33, 109
more أكثر **akthar** 50, 55
morning صباح **ṣabāḥ** 109
Morocco المغرب **al-maghrib** 118
Mr سيّد سادة **sayyid sāda** 34
Mrs سيّدة **sayyida** 34
much كثير **kathīr** 50
Muscat مسقط **masqaṭ** 118
museum متحف متاحف **matḥaf matāḥif** 50

N

name اسم اسماء **ism asmā'** 29
nation وطن أوطان **waṭan owṭān** 42
national وطني **waṭanī** 42
near قريب **qarīb** 50
necessary ضروري **ḍarūrī** 36; لازم **lāzim** 67
necessity ضرورة **ḍarūra** 35
new جديد جدد **jadīd judud** 73
news item خبر أخبار **khabar akhbār** 41, 59; أنباء نبأ **naba' anbā'** 24, 59
newspaper صحيفة صحف **ṣaḥīfa ṣuḥuf** 73; جريدة جرائد **jarīda jarā'id** 74
Nile نيل **nīl** 20
no لا **la** 15
north شمال **shimāl** 29
northern شمالي **shimālī** 29
notice إعلان **i9lān** 73
now الآن **al-'ān** 24
number رقم أرقام **raqm arqām** 49; نمرة نمر **numra numar** 99
nurse ممرّض\ممرّضة **mumarriḍ(a)** 84

O

objection احتجاج **iḥtijāj** 41
occasion مناسبة **munāsaba** 71
occupied محتلّ **muḥtall** 118
occupied territories الأراضي المحتلّة **al-'arāḍī l-muḥtalla** 118
office مكتب مكاتب **maktab makātib** 49, 60

official رسمي **rasmī** 73
officially رسمياً **rasmīyan** 51
oil نفط **nafṭ** 99
Oman عمان **9umān** 118
open مفتوح **maftūḥ** 49, 67
open! افتح **iftaḥ** 94
or أو **ow** 18
organisation تنظيم **tanẓīm** 42, 69; منظمة **munaẓẓama** 42

P

Pakistan باكستان **pākistān** 61
palace قصر قصور **qaṣr quṣūr** 92
Palestine فلسطين **filasṭīn** 118
Paris باريس **pārīs** 54
parking إيقاف **īqāf** 91; توقيف **touqīf** 91
parliament برلمان **barlamān** 92
participant مشترك **mushtarik** 68
participation اشتراك **ishtirāk** 70
particular خاص **khāṣṣ** 41
partition تقسيم **taqsīm** 50
passing مرور **murūr** 91
payment دفع مدفوعات **daf9 madfū9āt** 99
peace سلام **salām** 93
perfect تمام **tamām** 16
period مدة مدد **mudda mudad** 109
personal شخصي **shakhṣī** 73
photograph, picture صورة صور **ṣūra ṣuwar** 73
playground, playing-field ملعب ملاعب **mal9ab malā9ib** 50
please... الرجاء **ar-rajā'** 95
please do not... الرجاء عدم **ar-rajā' 9adam** 95
pleased مسرور **masrūr** 33
plumbing سباكة **sibāka** 62
police بوليس **būlīs** 91; شرطة **shurṭa** 42
policeman شرطي **shurṭī** 92
policy, politics سياسة **siyāsa** 99
poor فقير فقراء **faqīr fuqarā'** 50
possibility إمكانية **imkānīya** 50
possible ممكن **mumkin** 49
post وظيفة وظائف **waẓīfa waẓā'if** 84
pound (£) جنيه **jinayh** 109
present (not absent) حاضر **ḥāḍir** 67; موجود **moujūd** 84
presentation تقديم **taqdīm** 73
president رئيس رؤساء **ra'īs ru'asā'** 33

press صحافة **ṣiḥāfa** 73
price سعر أسعار **si9r as9ār** 44, 59
primary ابتدائي **ibtidā'ī** 37
principal رئيسي **ra'īsī** 37
printed مطبوع **maṭbū9** 62
private خاص **khāṣṣ** 41
problem مشكلة مشاكل **mushkila mashākil** 50, 60
production إنتاج **intāj** 41
professor أستاذ أساتذة **ustādh asātidha** 34
prohibited ممنوع **mamnū9** 62, 67, 91
proposal اقتراح **iqtirāḥ** 50, 55
proposed مقترح **muqtaraḥ** 68
public عامّ **9āmm** 44
public official مأمور **ma'mūr** 84
published منشور **manshūr** 50

Q

Qatar قطر **qaṭar** 118
quantity كمّية **kammīya** 50, 55
question سؤال أسئلة **su'āl as'ila** 29

R

Rabat الرّباط **ar-ribāṭ** 118
radio راديو **rādiō** 73
reading قراءة **qirā'a** 73
ready حاضر **ḥāḍir** 67; مستعدّ **musta9idd** 68
reasonable معقول **ma9qūl** 84
receiver مستقبل **mustaqbil** 68
reception استقبال **istiqbāl** 50, 70
recruitment استخدام **istikhdām** 70
Red Sea البحر الأحمر **al-baḥr al-'aḥmar** 118
reform إصلاح **iṣlāḥ** 71
registration تسجيل **tasjīl** 99
rejected مستنكر **mustankar** 68
rejection استنكار **istinkār** 50
relations علاقات **9alāqāt** 73
renewal تجديد **tajdīd** 71
repair تحسين **taḥsīn** 50
report تقرير تقارير **taqrīr taqārīr** 49, 61, 69
reporter مقرّر **muqarrir** 50, 67
representative ممثّل **mumaththil** 18, 67
represented ممثّل **mumaththal** 67
reserved محفوظ **maḥfūẓ** 67
resident ساكن سكّان **sākin sukkān** 50
responsible مسؤول **mas'ūl** 29
restaurant مطعم مطاعم **maṭ9am maṭā9im** 44

rial ريال **riyāl** 33
right(-hand) يمين **yamīn** 91
Riyadh الرّياض **ar-riyāḍ** 118
riyal ريال **riyāl** 33
road طريق طرق **ṭarīq ṭuruq** 91
Rome روما **rōma** 54

S

salary راتب رواتب **rātib rawātib** 84
Saudi Arabia السّعودية **as-sa9ūdīya** 118
school مدرسة مدارس **madrasa madāris** 34, 60, 62
Scotland اسكوتلندا **iskotlanda** 54
secondary ثانوي **thānawī** 17
see...! انظر **unẓur** 94
sender مرسل **mursil** 67
sent مرسل **mursal** 67
sewing خياطة **khiyāṭa** 62
short قصيرقصار **qaṣīr qiṣār** 73
shut! اقفل **iqfil** 94
sick مريض مرضى **marīḍ marḍa** 35
sign إشارة **ishāra** 91
slow down! تمهّل **tamahhal** 27, 94
small صغير صغار **ṣaghīr ṣighār** 50
smoking تدخين **tadkhīn** 91
socialism اشتراكية **ishtirākīya** 70
socialist اشتراكي **ishtirākī** 70
solid ثابت **thābit** 7
son ابن أبناء **ibn abnā'** 8
south جنوب **janūb** 41
southern جنوبي **janūbī** 41
speaking كلام **kalām** 50
special خاصّ **khāṣṣ** 41
specially خاصّةً **khāṣṣatan** 51
speech خطاب أخطبة **khiṭāb akhṭiba** 73; *(= speaking)* كلام **kalām** 50
speed سرعة **sur9a** 91
square ميدان ميادين **maydān mayādīn** 91
Stop! قف **qif** 49, 94
stopping وقوف **wuqūf** 91
street شارع شوارع **shāri9 shawāri9** 44
strike إضراب **iḍrāb** 35, 70
student طالب طلاّب **ṭālib ṭullāb** 68
study دراسة **dirāsa** 34
Sudan السّودان **as-sūdān** 118

sum مبلغ مبالغ **mablagh mabāligh** 44

sun شمس **shams** 29

Switzerland سويسرا **swisira** 54

Syria سوريا **sūriya** 36

T

tax ضريبة ضرائب **ḍarība ḍarā'ib** 99

tea شاي **shāy** 29

teacher معلّم **mu9allim** 44, 67; معلّمة **mu9allima** 68

technical فنّي **fannī** 48

telephone تلفون\تليفون **tilifōn/tilīfōn** 54

television تليفزيون **tilivizyūn** 73

tenant مستأجر **musta'jir** 68

text نصّ نصوص **naṣṣ nuṣūṣ** 73

thing شيء أشياء **shay' ashyā'** 29, 59

time وقت أوقات **waqt owqāt** 109

a time مرّة **marra** 33

today اليوم **al-youm** 99

tools آلات **ālāt** 15

tourism سياحة **siyāḥa** 62

town بلد بلاد **balad bilād** 91

town hall بلدية **baladīya** 92

trade تجارة **tijāra** 73

trader تاجر تجّار **tājir tujjār** 84

traffic مرور **murūr** 33

transfer انتقال **intiqāl** 71

transport نقل **naql** 91

traveller مسافر **musāfir** 67

Tripoli طرابلس **ṭarābulus** 118

tuition تعليم **ta9līm** 50, 69

Tunis(ia) تونس **tūnis** 118

turning مرور **murūr** 91

tutorial تعليمي **ta9līmī** 70

U

unemployment بطالة **baṭāla** 84

united متّحد **muttaḥid** 68, 118

university جامعة **jāmi9a** 92

urban مدني **madanī** 84

use استعمال **isti9māl** 50

useful مفيد **mufīd** 67

user مستعمل **musta9mil** 68

usually عادةً **9ādatan** 51

V

vegetation نبات **nabāt** 9

Vienna فيينا\ڤيينا **viyēna** 54

visit زيارة **ziyāra** 33

visitor زائر زوّار **zā'ir zuwwār** 62

voice صوت أصوات
ṣowt aṣwāt 35

W

wage أجر أجور **ajr ujūr** 84
wait(ing) انتظار **intiẓār** 70, 95
waiting for منتظر **muntaẓir** 68
warning تنبيه **tanbīh** 27
week أسبوع أسابيع
usbū9 asābī9 44, 60
west غرب **gharb** 44
western غربي **gharbī** 44
when لمّا **lamma** 19
where أين **ayna** 11
whose لمن **li-man** 19
work شغل أشغال
shughl ashghāl 84;
عمل أعمال
9amal a9māl 69, 84

worker, workman
عامل عمّال
9āmil 9ummāl 50, 62, 67
workshop مشغل مشاغل
mashghal mashāghil 50
world عالم عوالم
9ālam 9awālim 118
world(wide) عالمي **9ālamī** 84
writer كاتب كتّاب
kātib kuttāb 50, 62, 67
writing كتابة **kitāba** 69
written مكتوب
maktūb 50, 62, 67

Y

year سنة سنوات
sana sanawāt 29, 109
Yemen اليمن **al-yaman** 118

INDEX

The references are to page numbers. The sign '→' refers you to an entry with references.

Active → **Participle**

Adjective 36, 66, 74-78, 80, 103, 104, 113

Relative → **Relative**

Alphabet 2, 52, 53

Deep letters 8, 9, 14-16, 29, 32, 34, 40, 48

Disjoined letters 2, 5, 14-16, 26, 32, 33, 44

Doubled letters 18-20, 45

Joined letters 2, 6, 8, 9, 14, 15, 26, 28, 35, 40-44, 48, 49

Moon letters 21, 43

Shallow letters 6, 9, 15, 26, 28, 33, 35, 40, 48

Sun letters 20, 29, 32, 33, 42, 76

Tall letters 5-7, 14, 42

Teeth 10, 16, 32, 35, 41

Animate, Inanimate 77-80, 86

Article 19, 20, 24, 25, 29, 36, 45, 61, 76, 80, 100, 104

Command Form 94, 95

Consonant 9, 17, 27, 36, 45, 92

With dark sounds 34, 35, 42, 48

Construct (Basic Structure 3) 99-104, 113, 115

Definite (→ also **Article**) 19, 75-78, 80, 87, 95, 100-104, 113, 114

Description (Basic Structure 1) 74-78, 87, 88, 104

Dual → **Number**

Equation (Basic Structure 2) 85-88, 93-95, 104

Feminine → **Gender**

Gender 27, 37, 58, 61, 68, 74, 75, 77-80, 94, 110, 113

Handwriting 3, 71

Dots 6, 8, 9, 27, 101

Special shapes 10, 14-16, 26, 29, 32, 35, 41, 49, 50

Inanimate → **Animate**

Indefinite 36, 37, 77-79, 87, 101, 102, 104

Masculine → **Gender**

Noun 19, 36, 58-61, 66, 69, 70, 74-81, 86, 87, 92, 93, 99-103, 110, 112

Abstract 70

Proper 76, 100, 101

Relative → **Relative**

Verbal → **Verbal Noun**

Number (*singular/dual/plural;* → also **Animate**) 57-61, 68, 77, 78, 80, 81, 86, 95, 110, 112

Numbers (*1, 2, 3 …*) 62, 63, 109-114

One-letter word 25, 93

Participle 66-68

Passive → Participle
Plural → Number
Possessive 78-81, 85, 92, 100
Preposition 91-94, 103
Pronoun 84, 85, 87, 92-94
Relative 36, 37, 57, 58, 70, 74
Rule
Construct 100, 102
Doubled letter 18
Equation 86
Inanimate plural 77
Initial long vowel 11
Short vowel 7
Singular → Number
Stress 7, 8, 10, 20, 45, 113
Verbal Forms → Command Form, Participle, Verbal Noun
Verbal Noun 69, 95
Vowel 9, 17, 23, 36, 54
Dark 33, 41, 42, 48
Long 5, 6, 9, 10, 17, 18, 45, 54, 92
Short 2, 5, 7, 10, 18, 45, 51, 54, 92
Weak 25, 76

POCKET CARD

You may find it useful to make a pocket card from this page and carry it, for reference, when it is inconvenient to have the book with you. You can cut out the solid-line frame, fold it in half over a piece of card to stiffen it, and cover it with plastic film or heat-seal it in plastic for protection.

Alphabet

ا	alif	فـ ف	fā
بـ ب	bā	قـ ق	qāf
تـ ت	tā	كـ ك	kāf
ثـ ث	thā	لـ ل	lām
جـ ج	jīm/gīm	مـ م	mīm
حـ ح	ḥā	نـ ن	nūn
خـ خ	khā	هـ ـهـ ـه ه ـه	hā
د ذ	dāl dhāl	و	wow
ر ز	rā zayy	يـ ي ى	yā
سـ س	sīn		
شـ ش	shīn		
صـ ص	ṣād		
ضـ ض	ḍād		
ط ظ	ṭā ẓā		
عـ ـعـ ع ـع	9ayn		
غـ ـغـ غ ـغ	ghayn		

Variants and Signs

ء	’
ة	-a(t)
ى	-a
ًا ةً	-an, -atan
ّ...	*(doubling)*

Nouns (N) and Adjectives (A)

ة... -a(t), *f. s. (N/A); f. inan. pl. (A)*

ين...\ون... -īn/-ūn, *m. an. pl. (N/A)*

ات... -āt, *f.an.pl.(N/A); m./f.inan.pl.(N)*

Command, Participles, Vb. Nouns

اكتب uktub *write!*, اشرب ishrab *drink!*

كاتب kātib *writer*, مكتوب maktūb *written*

ممثّل mumaththil *represent/ative*, -al */-ed*

مساعد musā9id *assistant*

مرسل mursil *sender*, -al *sent*

منتخب muntakhib *elect/or*, -ab */-ed*

مستخدم mustakhdim *employ/er*, -am */-ed*

تفتيش taftīsh *inspection*

مساعدة musā9ada *help*

إرسال irsāl *despatch*

أنتخاب intikhāb *election*

استخدام istikhdām *employment*

Figures (→)

٠0 ١1 ٢2 ٣3
٤4 ٥5 ٦6
٧7 ٨8 ٩9